CONFESSION OF AN EMIGRANT

A MEMOIR

ELENA MIHAILA

Published by Mirran Books

Contact: mirran.books@gmail.com

This is a work of non-fiction. Some names and incidents have been changed to protect identities.

A catalogue record for this book is available from the National Library of New Zealand.

ISBN 978-0-473-63555-8 (paperback)
ISBN 978-0-473-63556-5 (EPUB)

CONTENTS

Foreword   vii

Chapter 1   1
Chapter 2   18
Chapter 3   36
Chapter 4   47
Chapter 5   55
Chapter 6   68
Chapter 7   74
Chapter 8   85
Chapter 9   96
Chapter 10   105
Chapter 11   113
Chapter 12   123
Chapter 13   135
Chapter 14   147
Chapter 15   158
Chapter 16   168
Chapter 17   185
Chapter 18   197
Chapter 19   212
Chapter 20   228
Chapter 21   248
Epilogue   255

Afterword   257
About the Author   261
Notes   263

*Each of us carries with us the story of a lifetime,
good and bad.*

FOREWORD

I have long been tormented by the thought that writing about my own troubles will not be of any interest to anyone. Yet, the desire and the hope that my confessions will be of help eventually convinced me to go further.

I am directing my words to the ones that wish to listen, especially to the ones for whom life has not always been generous.

I am not a literary writer, but I am a person who has battled with life, one who has suffered, and one who lives with the hope of the life that she desires, and I found myself capable to put all my experiences and related feelings on paper.

I have encountered malice when I was being kind, falsehood when I was being honest, and this has shaken my very core, even if the ache sprang only from the humility brought on by my own mistakes. I felt the ache of a reality that I had to face, and at my cries for help, I awoke my Faith.

For me, the testimony of a lifetime has a power of something HOLY; therefore, my confession is made in its entirety and with full confidence.

1

WE STEPPED OFF THE BUS INTO THE GLOOM OF A COLD, WET September evening. Two or three lamps hung from wooden posts, but their glow soon faded as we picked our way along the rough path to the village.

Soon we were in a darkness that was broken only by occasional pinpricks of light that seemed to float eerily among the trees. These were lanterns, carried by villagers whose errands had kept them out late and who were now heading home along the treacherous lanes. A dog barked in the distance, and was answered by another, then another even farther away.

We groped our way along, keeping a wary eye out for glints of mud and rain-filled potholes. I swapped my suitcase from one hand to the other, stumbling as I did so over an unseen root. Melancholy was fast becoming my first impression of my new home, and I could not help wondering if I was doing the right thing.

One by one our fellow travellers dropped off, prompted by some subtle mark or sign to turn through gates to their homes. I found myself almost resenting the warm hearths awaiting them. What for me was a forlorn and faintly hostile atmosphere was to them nothing more than a minor nuisance, a seasoning for the warm sustenance awaiting them at the end of their journey. I envied them their belonging. As an outsider, to whom everything was strange and new, all I could look forward to was unfamiliarity and absence – absence of the countless and pervasive shapes and smells and tastes of home that we only notice when they're gone.

By the time we reached the end of The Line, which I would learn this track through the village was called, Matei and I were alone. I let him lead while my head churned. What am I doing? Is this really me, walking this strange path? Leaving my whole life behind? Am I making a terrible mistake? Then I thought of my sons and felt my heart flood with longing and affection. I knew there was no going back from the road I'd chosen. Not ever. The die had been cast. Now I would find out the price I had to pay.

The track opened out and I could dimly make out a few dark houses. They looked uninhabited, with empty yards and broken fences. Here and there a roofed water well stood out. I imagined the chain and perhaps an old bucket hanging in the well mouth. Were people still living here? I wondered. Had Matei lost his way? Had I?

At last, we turned through a gate toward a house barely lit by a sickly bulb hanging over the porch. Matei opened the front door, but inside was no more inviting than out. Then, across the dark, cold hallway, I saw a faint crack of light. We climbed the two or three steps to the door and pushed it open.

I was immediately struck by the heat from within, making me aware how cold I had become. I could see the source of the warmth, an enormous stove in one corner of the room. Next to it was a bed, on which was perched an old woman in a nightdress. A kerchief was wound round her head and she held onto a cane.

"My God!" she said, looking up at our entrance. "Here they are!"

Matei's mother pushed herself to her feet amid joyful exclamations of reunion with her son, and hugged us both gleefully. When I could, I sat on the bed next to her. I was curious to take in some more of my new, temporary, home.

My first discovery was Matei's father. He was lying in the bed too, and though he'd said nothing yet, or perhaps because of that, I got the feeling he was on the crabby side of being reserved. But that could have just been his appearance, as he sat slowly chewing on his cigarette, appraising us. He held out his hand now, and I shook it, then he offered to light the fire in the room next door.

"It will warm up the room while we talk," he said, beginning to climb off the bed. But he didn't get to his feet. Instead, he let himself down onto the floor, and began to pull himself along with his hands.

Matei hadn't told me his father couldn't walk. I had known his parents were unwell, but I hadn't known the details. It was now becoming starkly clear just how little about my new life I knew, or had even thought about. In that small house, in that small village, I was amongst strangers. Not enemies, but not yet friends. How soon would that change? Had I tied myself to a future of caring for invalids? It was too soon to know. But this was what I had chosen. I had to live here now, with Matei's parents, to get to know them and have them get to know me. They were sick, but I could hardly hold that against them. Nor could I resent their close inspection of me. They were trying to understand who this new person was who had come into their lives, into their home, just as I was trying to understand where I was. Matei was their son, their only child, their hope for security in their old age. All they knew of me was that I had come with him on a brief visit, and that a short while later we were to move there permanently.

I didn't even know if they knew that I had left my husband, my sons, and resigned my job to be with Matei – who was about to leave the army. My parents had disowned us, and were unlikely to ever accept us back. All Matei and I could really be sure of was that we had a lot of struggle ahead of us before things would get easier. Perhaps his parents, frail as they were, could see that more clearly than we could, and perhaps that was behind their apparent reserve.

For my part, after the relief and joy I'd felt in escaping the intolerable conditions of home with Matei, my heart was now filling with sadness. Would it soon become remorse? I fought this fear down, and turned my mind back to the present, to Matei's village, his house, and his parents.

Matei's father had had a leg amputated several years previously, due to arthritis, but he had never been able to walk with the prosthetic limb the state provided him. He knew he wouldn't get another one. So, he simply stopped wearing it. He was too weak to use crutches, and a wheelchair was impossible in the house. So, in order to get around in his own house, he crawled.

Matei's mother could also barely move. She had suffered a stroke, and while she could talk clearly enough, her responses seemed only to highlight how harsh their life was, and how sad.

That evening, after discussing the usual pleasantries of the journey and the weather, I explained that we had only come for a few days. Matei had to report to his military unit in four days' time – although we both thought that he was likely to be dismissed when he did. Matei didn't care. It was pointless fighting it, so there was little to be gained from railing against the inevitable.

Instead, we had to focus on what we could change. I decided I would use my time with Matei's parents to do as much as possible to improve their home, even if it was only temporary. In the morning, I would see what an enormous task I was taking on. It was probably disrespectful to think so, but to tidy up a place that was as decrepit as its inhabitants would clearly take months of hard work, not just a few days.

As our conversation on that inauspicious night ground to a halt, Matei's mother suddenly cried out.

"But I can't see the difference between you!" she said, looking from her son to me and back. I think she was referring to our ages. At that time, in the late summer of 1986, I was thirty-nine and Matei was twenty-eight.

Her observation was a welcome relief to the tension, and I laughed along with her. Perhaps she had accepted us, our relationship and our situation. That made me think that maybe things would not be so bad after all.

It would be another year before we finally moved back to the village named Mircea cel Bătrân (Mircea the Elder, named for a fourteenth century Romanian ruler). It was a place as remote and forgotten by time and the rest of the country as Romania was by the rest of the world. Growing up in the southern city of Olteniţa, on the bank of the Danube, my father and I had often jokingly been called *ţăran*, or peasants. This was not from any great affinity we showed with rural activity, farming, or even gardening. It was because often, under various pretexts, my father would often take a train into the countryside, getting off in some village or other, and more often than not I would tag along with him.

In summers full of dust and heat we would sit on the benches between the train carriages, where the doors were always open, and feel as if we were flying above the fields and settlements. Crops, trees, houses, orchards, steeples, animals – all paraded before our eyes in a ceaseless colourful flow.

We would get off the train at random, anywhere that my father had friends or acquaintances, or that simply took his eye, and roam through the alleys in the heat of the summer sun. My father was the head of a large state tobacco packaging firm. While he stopped to talk with a villager – about the weather, the harvest, the prices of crops – I would glance over the fence at a flower garden, or watch hens bathing in the dust under the shade of a tree. Occasionally, a dog would appear from behind the house or the cool side of a garden shed and measure me up, too drowsy to bark. Sometimes we were invited indoors, where we would always be treated to a welcome glass of water, drawn cool from the well and usually accompanied by homemade fruit preserves.

They were peaceful, quiet, blessed days. And they were the sum total of my experience of rural life before I moved to Mircea cel Bătrân.

As we had expected, Matei's future in the army was finished. We rented rooms in a small town while he worked his time out, and when it came time to leave, we set out on Matei's sturdy Russian bicycle, which he nicknamed 'the Ferrari'. It must have been the only Ferrari in the world without a motor, and with a sidecar. We slung all our possessions on the handlebars, and while Matei pedalled, I sat in the sidecar with a bagful of books, reading aloud or working on crossword puzzles. Every now and then we stopped for a bite to eat, or to stretch our legs. Around three in the afternoon, tired, dusty and overwhelmed by the heat, we rode through the outskirts of the village where we were to live for the next three years.

Matei's parents didn't ask too much about his decision to leave the army. They knew he was independent and quick-tempered, and in any case, it was much to their advantage having us move in. For my part, I thought that, as long as Matei and I were together, things would work out.

The only gap that remained in my life, I thought at the time, was my two boys. The longing hadn't lessened by then. It never would. It was, is and in some shape and form always would be, a hole, an aching emptiness lodged in my heart. In the end I had had no choice but to flee my former home. But I could not help feeling that I should have been strong, stronger than I was; that I should have faced the situation I had created – no matter how hard that was.

But I didn't really have time to properly examine what I was doing. Everyone's desire to tell me what they thought was best, what I should do, to stop me doing what I felt was right and so to make my life even more unbearable than it was, had forced me down this path of the absolutely unknown. And of course, my own desire, my own weakness, was pulling me on. I couldn't resist.

Adding to my guilt had been what my family did to Matei. Forcing him out of the army, depriving us of work and money, they thought that eventually he would find I wasn't worth it. He would give me up and I would have to come crawling back. But their plans failed. Matei and I stayed together, choosing to make a life together in a small village that could not have changed much in the past three hundred years. Village life was a life I knew nothing about. But we were at least together.

The village of Mircea cel Bătrân sits in the midst of the broad fertile plains of eastern Romania, known as the Bărăgan. It had less than a hundred houses then, and, like so many similar villages across Europe, it had been steadily abandoned by its youngsters, who had headed to the cities and the imagined luxury of regular work, a fixed salary, or the same thing Matei and I sought: a chance to escape. If they came back to the village, I could see in them the same mixed emotions and behaviours that Matei and I had. They were neither city folk nor peasants any more. The great majority of people who remained in the village were aged over forty and worked hard for a life that didn't seem to offer much in return. Yet the village itself never seemed to be ailing or in decline, and in time, I would learn why.

Having returned for good, we rested for a few days, and then I took stock of the place we had decided to live in. We had to make plans for the changes needed to make the household work. The main house, the outbuildings, the yard, everything needed urgent repairs, and everything had to be done in the space of a few months, before the worst of winter arrived. Once the homestead was running properly, we thought that we would look for work.

I wondered how to make sure the changes would please everyone. At the front of the house was the large room and entrance hall where Matei's parents had first received us. In its glory days the room would have been the winter kitchen, but it served well enough now as a bedroom for Matei's parents because of the large stove. Adjoining it was another room, used as the grain store. Outside that was a shed, with an earthen stove. This was where cooking would be done in summer, both because of the unwelcome heat and the ability to burn wood rather than gas.

Between the domestic buildings was an attractive arbour, formed by four poles supporting grape vines. Here was a chance to create something nice. We built another oven there for baking, and put in a long table and bench, so in summer we could chat with our neighbours over glasses of wine and beer, and dishes of fried bread or popcorn.

There were more changes to make. The poultry yard, vegetable garden, flower garden, sheds, storage barrels, even the house we were to live in, everything was in need of a helping hand. We soon learned to ask our neighbours for help with planning the repairs and carrying them out.

The locals had eyed me cautiously when I arrived, probably wondering how this newcomer, this city lady, would cope with real work, and how long it would be before I gave up. But they were curious, too, to know what we were up to. And as the property took shape, they would find one excuse or another to come and see for themselves. "She is a *haiduc*,[1] this lady," they would tell Matei's parents, "not a woman. She doesn't stop!"

It took us three months of working dawn to dusk, but the results were beyond my expectations. After a day's work we would wash, using the bucket and the earthen jug perched on a shelf off the fence. Then we would wander to the far edges of the village, gradually getting a feel for its contours, its features, the dusty hollows and crooked palings and the rhythms of life of the land and its inhabitants. We would see villagers who had returned from a day's work in the fields, now busy around their homes. In summer, they would cook and dine outside, as we did, under a shed or a tree. As day slowly mixed into night, you could hear them commenting on the events of the day, or calling a child to fetch a bundle of corn husks for the fire, or tending to the chickens and other farm animals.

These neighbourhood rambles were part of the vital process of getting to know our new home, and adapting to its ways. Often, we would find ourselves stopping by the home of distant relatives of Matei's parents, whom we called Auntie Tinca and Uncle Toader. This wonderful couple invited me into their home shortly after I first arrived in Mircea cel Bătrân, and during the whole time I was there stood beside me like parents and friends.

Tinca was only a little over sixty, but a life of hard work she said she had been "greedy" for had permanently bent her body. She was full of wisdom and common sense, was both serious and humane, and embodied what for me was the essence of the Romanian peasant. She reminded me that we were in fact a rural people, and that our great intellectual values had originated from these sensibilities. I was proud of her friendship, and I believe it was from her that I learned much about the kind of strength I would need on the journey ahead.

Despite her back, Tinca was herself a *haiduc*, on the go from morning till evening. Her house was clean as a whistle, inside and out. The poultry run, flower garden and front yard were all as meticulously and skilfully cared for as her living room. The furniture inside had dozens of coverlets, all of which she had woven on her loom, along with stacks of rugs and comforters. These were intended as dowries for her children and grandchildren.

She and Uncle Toader had three children, two of whom already had families of their own. The youngest, Coca, still lived at home, and taught at one of the schools in a neighbouring village.

Tinca had an incredible memory. Uncle Toader would come in, tired and dusty after a day's work, complaining about how he was looking forward to retirement and having nothing to do but a few household chores. Then Tinca would begin, "You know, it was in 1939, on a Sunday, about three in the afternoon," and then proceed to tell us of some remark of Toader's or an event tied quite specifically to that date.

We spent many pleasant evenings, together with Coca, listening to Tinca's stories and catching up on the village news. I never quite knew what Toader was thinking as he studied me silently from beneath his thick brows. Some years later he told me, "How beautiful you were, Elena." If that was all, I wouldn't have minded if he'd told me at the time!

As Matei and I headed home late in the evening, the lanes were brightly lit by the moon rising from the shadows of the forest, weaving a magical silence we didn't dare interrupt. It was all a far cry from that chilly night that was my introduction to Mircea cel Bătrân and village life. But one thing was unchanged from that day and every day – my longing for my boys. I knew I had hurt them, and I couldn't forgive myself. The thought that they suffered because of me poisoned my soul, and I couldn't find peace. I was bitterly upset that I had left Remus, my eldest son, just as he was about to take his university exams. It was no help at all to him that I was beside him in my thoughts and in my soul. Often despair took hold of me, and I would lock myself inside the house, where without being seen I would cry and writhe like an injured animal, hoping to relieve the deep, excruciating pain in my breast.

As the days came and went, some opportunities did arise to fill that hole. When I found out when the exam results would be posted, I ran to the next village, where there was a telephone, impatient to find out. Through family friends in Bucharest, I found my boy had passed the entrance exam for medical school. I was so overjoyed that I cried and laughed my way home, barely resisting the urge to tell everyone I passed why I was so happy.

Then, towards the evening of one autumn day, I had just lit the fire when a knock came at the door. Standing there was Dragos, my youngest boy, with a friend of my mother's. With his eyes pleading louder than his words, he begged me to come home. "Please," he said, "I promise I'll protect you. No one will hit you again!"

I was dumbstruck. I stood like a statue, unable to utter a single word, feeling the hot and bitter tears gushing from my heart. Here at last my wish had been granted, to see my son, and I could not speak to him. I was terrified that if I started talking, I would tell him what I myself had only just learned; I was pregnant.

Where the strength came from to stand motionless on the doorstep and just say, "I will always be here for you and Remus. But I cannot come home," I don't know. But that was all I could do. A few days later, I learned that Remus would do his military service in Moldova, which was a province in the north of the country. At least there, I thought, I should be able to visit him.

Meanwhile, we became increasingly settled. We brought furniture in and the house began to look good: there was a large bedroom, a dining room, a kitchen, and we created a nursery. I had met most of our neighbours and Matei's relatives. His father had three sisters in the village, and they had been a great help since our arrival. It was now time to start thinking about finding some productive work. I had qualified as an agricultural engineer and had a background in tobacco from working at the factory my father ran. I thought it should not be too difficult to find some kind of job in the local farm cooperative. One morning, as I was walking down the main road to the neighbouring village, the man whom I knew was the head of the local council stopped me.

"I heard you were new around here," he said, after introducing himself. You know, we want to reopen the store in Mircea cel Bătrân. We thought you might be interested in managing it."

I thanked him and explained that my background wasn't really suited for that. Instead, I was hoping to find something to do in one of the agricultural cooperatives in the district. Of course, I could take on something else if necessary, but working as a store manager probably wasn't really my strength.

"Oh, don't let that stop you," he said. "Look at me. I used to be a tractor driver and now I am a mayor."

On my way home I was reminded of a joke my father had told me. A man with no skills but quick wits and a bit of luck had become very wealthy. For some reason he appeared in court, and when the judge asked him his occupation, he answered 'millionaire'. "That's not a proper occupation," the judge said. "It might not be," the rich man replied. "But it's *so* good!" Something about the arrogance of that response reminded me of the village mayor's attitude.

A few evenings later I was at our gate as people were making their way home from the fields, when the manager of the district farm stopped his gig in front of me.

"I hear you want my job," he said bluntly.

I was taken aback, but I ignored his tone of voice and instead

simply told him my situation. I was looking for work, I said, but
would be having a child soon and under no circumstances had I set
my sights on his job. I was hoping to find something convenient
that would allow me to work but still be near the baby.

He calmed down a little after that and stayed a while to talk. I
gathered that even though I hadn't approached the leaders of the
agricultural co-op to ask about work, the answer had already been
decided, and it was, "No".

But my interest was piqued now. Some days later I decided to
formally inquire at the county agricultural headquarters about
work. I learned that they were planning to replace the accountant
of our village farm. He was long past retirement age, and as it
turned out he had never held the right qualifications for the job
anyway.

I left a job application addressed to the co-op leaders. Three
weeks later I had had no response. The office was six or seven
kilometres away, so I decided to go and see if I could find out what
was going on. Just as I arrived, I spied the co-op chairman about to
leave.

"It's not possible," he said, when I asked him about my
application. "We have an accountant." He climbed into his car.

"But I have the approval of the agricultural leadership," I said,
stretching the truth to breaking point in my desperation.

"Impossible. Our accountant is the godfather of the farm
manager. They get along fine. Do you understand? There's
nothing you can do."

I knew I needed help, and thought I might know where to find
it. I left the place feeling so angry that I was able to flag down a
truck that was passing. I asked the driver to drop me at The
Crosses, the closest intersection to the county Communist Party
offices.

It was called "The Crosses" because there was a group of

ancient crosses there, leaning and half buried in the ground. It was
not all that unusual to see such relics here and there in the fields of
the Bărăgan. Ploughs eager to sink their greedy fangs into the
fertile soil somehow stayed clear of them. Many looked as if they
had been there from time immemorial, and, as I had always been
attracted by mysteries, every time I saw one I would inspect it. It
was fascinating trying to understand the signs that had been
almost completely obliterated by winds and rain, wondering what
their reason for existence had been. Some people thought they had
helped to guide shepherds bringing down their flocks from the
mountains for winter, followed by a procession of wagons, dogs,
donkeys, and their families. I imagined how wild these places must
have looked back then, when wagon wheel ruts and the tracks
beaten by the small, sharp hooves of sheep were the only marks
left on the earth.

At the party headquarters, I was determined to see the local
secretary. Nobody else would have the authority I needed. I had
heard people refer to this man by a name that sounded familiar,
and I decided to back my hunch. An hour later, I knew I hadn't
been wrong. Twenty years earlier, the man had held the same
position in my home town. It didn't take long to establish the
connection, and he invited me to tell him why I was there.

There was a position for an accountant on our village farm, I
explained. I had applied, but the farm cooperative leadership
wouldn't accept me. I had the experience, I was expecting a baby,
and I would be able to work from Mircea cel Bătrân without
affecting the regular work of the cooperative.

Calmly, he invited me to sit down and tell him the latest news
from Oltenița, of which he still held fond memories. Finally, he
told me to go home and not to worry, assuring me that I would be
hired.

Another two weeks passed without any news. So, I went back to the party secretary.

"What is it?" he asked, a little puzzled to see me again so soon.

"Nobody called," I replied. "Nothing happened."

He asked me to wait in the reception area, where I overheard him calling someone on the telephone. Before long a man rushed past me and went through the secretary's office.

It was impossible not to overhear. "What are you doing, man? I told you to hire that lady on the co-op farm. Why didn't you? Does it take a whip to make you listen?"

There was nowhere for me to hide. But it wasn't my fault. Maybe it wasn't his either; I suspected that strings were being pulled by the co-op leadership, a clique that didn't want to get separated.

A few minutes later the man came out of the office and introduced himself.

"My name is Aron, the chief of the agricultural directorate. You should have come directly to me about this. But no matter. You're hired now."

There seemed little point reminding him that this was what I'd been told a few weeks previously.

This time, though, it worked. And so, I started work as a farm accountant. I was pregnant and there was a lot to do at home, so it was very convenient to be able to work in the village. Being late autumn, there were only a small number of men on fieldwork. The women worked in my office, a huge room with a terracotta fireplace that warmed the place nicely on cold days. Sitting around the long table in the centre of the room, they sorted seeds for the spring plantings. I got to know about many of the villagers at that table, as we chatted while we worked.

I soon learned that the farm boss said he was satisfied with the new arrangement, and that even the old accountant didn't seem to bear a grudge over what had happened. So, for a time at least, Matei's and my life seemed secure.

Around this time, through the help of old friends of the family, I arranged to visit Remus in Moldova, where he was completing his military service. He was stationed in a town called Focşani. Matei accompanied me to the train station, where an old family friend Vetuţa and her husband, Mircea, had done everything they could to try and reconcile my parents and me. Foreseeing the kind of difficulties we would have, they'd also tried their best to convince me to give up my plans to leave. But, unlike my family, they'd been able to accept my decision, and so it was wonderful to share my joy at the prospect of seeing my eldest son with Vetuţa. I left her talking with Matei at the station and stepped onto the train that was taking me to see my boy.

My boy! The uniform made him look like a man. But I knew that under those rough clothes was a delicate and sensitive soul I had caused to suffer so much. It was wonderful to spend time in his company, and together we laughed and told stories. But, no matter how I tried to ignore it, the pain was there. The pain of being apart from him, that I wasn't there when he came home at the weekend, and that I wasn't the first to share all the changes taking place in his life as a student. I tried to tell myself that such thoughts were useless, that what was done was done. He only had six months to serve, I thought, and after that I would be able to see more of him.

The train home was full, and I sat in a corner listening to the conversations around me, about families, jobs and, as always, criticisms of the government. Suddenly, somebody spoke to me.

"Do you have children?"

"Two boys, both over eighteen. And one on the way."

"So young and with grown-up children!"

Was I young? I hadn't thought in a long time of how I looked, but the remark pleased me. I would soon be forty and I was going to have a baby! I had never thought that it might be too late. I started to worry then about what could go wrong with having a child so late, but luckily the train arrived, and Matei was waiting for me. As soon as I started to tell him about my trip I cheered up, as he shared heart and soul in my own joy.

2
_____

THE VILLAGERS WERE GETTING TO KNOW ME NOW, AND IT seemed they almost accepted me. And I came to know their lives. I lived amongst them, learning their customs, their secrets, their sufferings and their joys. There was no question life had been miserly with them, that they had far too few of the gifts and joys intended for humankind. They were simple folk with not much education, modest, hardworking. They belonged to that company of workers you will find all over the world, who perform the hard, unsung labour of daily toil. Whether as office workers, or farm workers, or employed in the village, they were the cogs that kept the big wheels turning, and were completely unacknowledged and unrewarded.

Those times in Romania were of course highly distressing. Working-class people seemed resigned to a life full of more hardship than joy, knowing full well their work was keeping others at a level of comfort and ease they themselves could not even dream of. They were exhausted by their hard work, and any time I could, I would help them. Many times I left in a wagon for the fields and, protected by the guards who helped me without question, brought back a bag full of produce I knew they were short of. It wasn't legal – it was stealing from the state, I suppose – but it seemed to me against the laws of nature that these people should be paid so little for their work. Especially when all the while their bosses took more than they needed, so they could look after their families and relatives, as well as paying for their easy chairs. And so on up the line it went.

When we first arrived in Mircea cel Bătrân, I was told that if ever I needed honey, to visit Mr. Costica, the retired schoolteacher. He lived a few doors away, and when I did eventually knock on his door, I was welcomed by his wife, whose beautiful face was framed by thick, white hair.

"Oh, you are Madame Elena," she greeted me, smiling. "I heard you'd settled here in the village. We very much admire your courage, you know, and especially the way you've coped with moving here."

I was still processing this somewhat backhanded compliment when Mr. Costica appeared. He had a strong, intelligent face and radiated energy and a strong will. The villagers had told me that almost all of them had been taught by him at one time or another. Meeting him in person I felt a strong sense of admiration for this man who, I had heard, had built a reputation amongst the villagers for honesty and for speaking the truth, all the while managing to elude persecution. After our first meeting we often met on the path leading to the adjoining village or on mornings when he was taking his geese to pasture. Each time, I stopped with pleasure to exchange a few words with him.

One evening, well after sunset, Matei stopped outside our house in a car. He was with a friend, a village teacher, and they were on a mission to pick up some watermelons. I couldn't help myself, and went along with them. It was after 10pm when we headed off, armed with a bottle of plum brandy, which we knew would be more than a match for the local guards, and a note from the chief engineer of the co-op, stating we were each entitled to ten melons. Arriving at the melon field, we found two guards. One was friendly enough, but the other was already drunk. Apparently somebody had got there before us, and his eyes were cold as we showed him our official letter. We got on with loading the melons, however, when suddenly he started shouting.

"Stop! Stop! Don't take any more! Put those melons down. Get out of here!"

Trying to pacify him, we explained again that we had a document from the co-op leadership. But it was no use. He wouldn't listen, and kept insisting that we put the melons back and leave. So we stopped trying to talk sense to him, got into the car and drove off with what we had, leaving him behind screaming and waving.

Some distance along the track we glimpsed another car's headlights. Our first thought was they were most likely more melon aficionados like ourselves. We were surprised then when the car stopped in front of us and four young men got out. In the light of the headlamps we could see that each of them was carrying a knife. I was imagining myself being dragged away somewhere into the darkness, but Matei, in an inspired manoeuvre, took off as fast as he could. He just squeezed past their car, then we headed at full speed for the village. Matei knew the road well, and by the time they turned their car round a thick dust cloud rose behind ours that restricted their vision. We were not far from the village when our pursuers finally gave up.

The next day, in conversation with our local police captain, I learned that two of our four pursuers were the drunken guard's sons. Guards were able to get away with pretty much anything, he said, because it was hard to find people to stay there at night, in the middle of the field, until the end of the season.

"We need tough men," he concluded, although it wasn't clear if he meant that guard was, in his view, part of the solution or part of the problem.

Later, when I had got used to how things worked in the village, I would sometimes head to the stables at five in the morning, harness the horses to one of the wagons, and head off alone to one of the melon fields. From there I usually returned with a wagonload of fruit, in exchange, naturally, for the bottle which I always had handy. I would then share my plunder with everyone I knew.

My upbringing taught me that a good householder stays by the hearth in winter, prepared for whatever the weather brings. I wanted to get properly organised. I wanted to see my pantry full of preserves, the bins full of flour and grains for the poultry and animals, and the woodshed full. And I wanted to make wine and plum brandy.

Everyone in the village would get involved in harvesting the vineyards tracing the lower reaches of the hills and encircling the heart of the village. For two days nobody worked in the fields and the village looked like a beehive, full of the buzzing of old and young alike, from dawn till nightfall. At the end of each plot of vines, now coloured in rust by autumn, the wagons waited, carrying the presses that would be filled with juicy grapes. Children skipped and hopped about impatiently, waiting for the uncorking so that they could drink the cloudy, sticky, sweet juice.

Our vineyard hadn't been well cared for. It was past pruning time when we first arrived, and for that reason we didn't have a very rich harvest. But even so we were content with what we did produce.

We hadn't fared much better with the corn either, so one afternoon I left Matei by himself in the vineyard, and, finding a free wagon, went uphill to where the agricultural cooperative's vegetable garden was. I took a roomy shoulder bag with me, and headed towards the plateau at the end of the village, where besides other crops the rich cornfields swayed. I filled my bag, but as I was leaving the rows I met the field guard. He was part of a team of workers the co-op had hired down from the mountainous regions to help with autumn harvest work, and he didn't know who I was.

"What are you doing?" he asked.

"I took some corn for my poultry," I answered.

He seemed taken aback by my honesty. "Oh. You're not afraid to admit it? Even though you know it's not allowed?"

"I know, but I haven't been here long. What else can I do? The chickens will starve if I don't do something."

"Okay," said the man, looking around. "But go quickly in case somebody sees you. Some of these guys will put you in prison for an ear of corn."

Yes, I did know that, just as I knew that the humble were usually prosecuted while the rich were not, often to cover up for those in power, to conceal the fact that they used the people's wealth as their own. Not everyone treated their fellow humans like animals, though. A few days later, the same man, together with his teammates, came to my office to check on his work assignment. He recognised me and was surprised to see me, but didn't let on. I could see he was glad he had helped me, and I thanked him again with a glance.

The bag of corn wasn't enough to solve my problem, however. I had to find something else, another way to stock up on grains for the poultry until high winter came, when produce would be shared out by the cooperative.

Fortunately, a solution almost fell into my lap. The mountain workers were paid partly in cash but mostly in kind. Some of them had come with wagons to help carry back their compensation, in particular corn. As luck would have it, the route of the chain of wagons, which could hardly move under the weight, passed right in front of our gate. Each of the wagon masters offered to help me with a few ears of corn that, with just a little push, slid down from the golden piles shining in the autumn sunlight.

One morning I was woken by a strong wind beating against the windows. My annoyance was quickly followed by a single idea: walnuts. In a field some seven or eight kilometres from the village stood a walnut plantation. It was a remnant from the orchard that was part of the estate of the former landowner. The trees had shaded the houses and other outbuildings of the main house. The buildings had long gone, but the magnificent walnut trees were still there.

The lowest branches were so high you couldn't reach them with a stick. It was only when a strong wind came that the walnuts would fall, and though he wasn't an early riser, Matei also knew an opportunity when it came along. Soon we were off in the morning darkness. That evening I counted over six thousand walnuts.

I was now prepared for the winter: the wine was bubbling, the pantry was full, the plum brandy was made, the yard was full of poultry. Later, in winter, we would spend our weekends around the samovar in which we heated the wine, playing cards with Coca. There were always homemade biscuits, and when Matei saw Coca appear around the corner on her way to us he would open the window to let her hear him call out to me, "Quick, Elena, hide the baking – Coca is coming."

Coca would laugh at the teasing, a joyful sound that always delighted me. She was a smart girl, and pretty, but unfortunately, due to a childhood disease, suffered a bad limp. I admired her for the courage with which she faced life. She knew her situation and her prospects, she didn't expect anything to be offered to her on a tray, and she took for herself what she considered her due. Somehow, all that seemed to be captured in that laugh.

There were many good times, in that first year in Mircea cel Bătrân. By the time winter settled in, Dragos was visiting me pretty often. Remus had just a short time left in his military service. I felt good at home. I found joy in work of any kind and only rarely needed to leave the village that had become my home. When I did, especially in winter, it was a journey fraught with unusual risk. On one trip to the neighbouring village, I was unable to return until well after dark. My shearling coat barely reached my waist, but I was thankful for its warmth nevertheless. Then, as I was entering my village, two large dogs bounded from the yard of a house. In a second, I was hurled down in a snowdrift. The coat protected my skin from their teeth, but I got a huge fright. Returning from another trip, this time forty kilometres away to the nearest city, I got off at the station ten kilometres away from our village. Normally the train was met by the bus that picked up workers for a nearby factory.

Unfortunately, though not unusually, the train had been late, and I was one of a group of about twenty passengers left in an open field, met by a howling snowstorm such as can only happen in the Bărăgan. We were a group waiting for a miracle. Then, one happened. A passing truck stopped, and the driver, a local, insisted on taking every one of us.

When we got down a furious wind was hurling snow in every direction. It pricked our eyes with its stinging needles. The snow reached to our knees, and though I was heavily pregnant I trudged through it, determined not to lag behind. Suddenly, through the wind-driven snow, torchlight fell on my face. It was Dragos. He had arrived earlier, found an unlocked window, entered and lit the fire. Home at last, and when I had recovered from my ordeal, Dragos spent the night telling me about his girlfriend, Carmen. He promised he would soon bring her to meet me.

Heavy snow fell around Christmas and the unfailing north wind (Crivăț) wreaked havoc in the village, penetrating every nook and cranny, running along the paths, whistling harshly, beating unmercifully on anything in its way. And still I loved it. The wind blew from mysterious places known and seen by it alone, the snow was what made Christmas trees so beautiful, and filled the children's holidays with the charming uproar of sled runs. These scenes triggered a longing to be in touch with home, and so once again I headed towards the neighbouring village and the telephone office, this time with Matei. My family still weren't talking to me, so I called Vetuța to get the news. I knew my mother was suffering because of what had happened, and that she would never accept what I had done, but I was still grateful to her and my father for the care they had taken of my sons.

I entered the telephone office leaving behind a frosty but quiet winter evening. When I came out an hour later, it was into a full-blown snowstorm. The wind, snow and especially the ice that glistened all around, like an immense mirror, made us stumble. A thick fog prevented us from seeing more than a couple of feet in front of us. We held hands trying to make our way through the darkness and fog, under the stinging ice hurled at our faces by the wind. It seemed as if the spirits of the sky were fighting one another, and we yelled to make ourselves heard over their roaring, howling battle.

We had heard rumours that during harsh winters, when blizzards such as this swept over the countryside, wild wolves and boars would leave their thickets near the villages and come right up to people's houses, seeking the warmth leaking from houses and barns. Despite Matei's assurances that such things hadn't happened for a long while, I was exceedingly frightened.

At long last, after the hours it took us to walk just a few kilometres, we made it home. Bathing in the welcome heat radiating from our stove, I couldn't help thinking how harsh these places must have been not too long ago.

Christmas meant it was time for Moş Crăciun, the Romanian Father Christmas, and the carols, rich meals, sweet breads, and joy that came with it. We decorated the tree outside in the yard, and I would sit late at night looking through the window at the coloured glow that could scarcely break through the thick snow covering its branches. This bewitching atmosphere was also very much a part of Christmas time, when you feel you can be a better, more generous person, and when you see a friend in everybody.

I had finished the housecleaning but still had the pig-butchering to do. The last week before Christmas, the whole village was frantic with the squealing of animals that seemed to know their fates, with people running to and fro, and with chores that seemed to have accumulated faster than ever. Everybody wanted to have their table laden with treats, their house well heated, the wine and plum brandy ready and their traditional pastries made. The smells wafting from oven doors were enough to send passers-by hurrying home to see what delights lay waiting for them.

I was up late finishing my Christmas Eve chores, but the next day was up at dawn to wait for the little carolers. "Good Morning, Christmas Eve" sung in crystal clear, innocent voices, full of hope that they would be met by generous householders, set my memory going. I remembered myself with my own little bag, sewn by grandma, and seven or eight friends all outfitted the same, ready to start carolling. We would not return until lunch, with our feet frozen, our hands and cheeks red with cold, and our bags full of pretzels, apples, and candy, all extremely happy.

As ever, the day after the Christmas and New Year festivities were over, everything went back to normal, and the habitual daily routine settled back in. This year, however, I was pregnant, and it was getting harder and harder for me to go to work every day. With no change in the relationship between my mother and me, comments among villagers about how odd it was my mother had never come to see me started to come more frequently. To quieten down the rumours, Vetuţa paid us a few days' visit, and played the role of my mother to anyone who cared to ask.

Early on my name day, the day of the emperor saints Constantin and Elena, my neighbour Ioana brought me a freshly picked bouquet of peonies. I remember thinking I had had two beds full of the white, red and pink flowers at home that were always in bloom on this day, and what a colourful and fragrant gift of nature they were – when the unforgettable pains of labour put all such memories aside.

As the contractions grew stronger Matei wanted to alert the county hospital. But I said no, and sent him to bring the village midwife instead. Coca and my neighbour, Baba Ioana, spun in circles in front of the window, but I didn't want to see anybody. I drew the curtains and sent them home. I didn't want to be heard as I screamed with the pain, though I later learned that I could be heard from the public fountain down the road, where people stopped to water their horses. Consequently, the news I was giving birth soon spread like wildfire.

The midwife and Matei stayed beside me. Around nine in the evening the county hospital midwife showed up, with an ambulance. I don't know who had contacted her, but she arrived firmly determined to take me to the hospital. I tried to get up, but the pains were now so frequent and strong that I collapsed back on the bed. "It's better for her to stay," I heard someone say. "The baby will be here in ten minutes."

"It's a girl!" I heard Matei cry out joyfully. "And she looks like me – hope you don't mind!" He ran out to share the news with his parents, but in his excitement he took off down the wrong path. Soon he poked his head back in.

"I forgot to ask if she has all her parts? As there are no spares available." The question, though lightly asked, was serious. The truth was I had tried everything to not have this child, and had only stopped when Matei found me out. "What are you doing?" he cried. "Can't you see that it is meant to be? Stop it!"

I named her Elena-Anca.

Around August I resumed work. I would leave Anca alone in her crib until mealtimes when I returned to feed her. After a few months one of the neighbours offered to take care of her while I was at work. I was soon hearing, "Madam, Anca had polenta with pickles today," or "She enjoys her fried pork." Despite such a diet, or perhaps because of it, who knows, Anca grew big and strong.

By now my boys were living in a Bucharest apartment with fellow university students, and were able to visit me more frequently. Both of them now had girlfriends called Carmen. Remus's Carmen was at university with him. Dragos soon married his Carmen, and she came with him whenever he visited us.

It was on one of those visits that Dragos surprised me by saying, "Mum, we have to leave the country. And we have to leave together. I'm not leaving without you."

My surprise was mainly because I had been having similar thoughts myself. I hadn't confessed them to anyone, though. I hadn't really taken the idea seriously anyway, with little Anca being so young. And I hadn't the slightest idea of how to do such a thing, which at the time represented an enormous risk. So much so it was almost shocking hear the idea said out loud.

Then I had a dream that seemed to confirm it was in fact my only choice.

Our house lay on six acres of land, and on it, not far from our place, lived Matei's grandfather, his mother's father. Everyone called him the Old Man. He was well over ninety years old, and preferred to live alone with his memories and thoughts. We only saw him when he came for his three daily meals or occasionally to catch up with news from the village.

In my dream, Anca, Matei and I were in the middle of the road in front of our house, frightened, looking towards the hill at the edge of the village. From there a huge creature, like the giants I imagined in my childhood fairytales, was striding toward the Old Man's house. Immensely high, his head lost in the sky, this creature crushed his little house like a walnut. In one step he was in front of us, then he swept us up into his arms and flew into the sky. When I woke up my first thought was that the Old Man was going to die, but I didn't understand what the dream meant for us. A few months later, just before Christmas, we found the Old Man dead in his bed. There was snow on the ground, and a stone-splitting frost, on the day that we and just a very few others accompanied him on his last trip.

These few unsettling events aside, we had a quiet life with which I was largely content. But there was one growing cause of unhappiness: Matei's drinking. It wasn't just a few glasses, which wouldn't have bothered me, but he drank excessively, every day. Then he would wander about aimlessly, doing nothing useful, until well after midnight. I wasn't one for midnight feasts, nor for time wasting. Of course he was only human, and I didn't expect perfection, but with this happening night after night it began to go from being a nuisance to increasingly unbearable. I didn't want anything to muddy the contentment we were enjoying, but after a few failed attempts to address his behaviour, I began to look at everything with an angry helplessness.

When Anca could walk, I decided I needed a break, and took her home to meet her grandparents. Somewhere in my soul I clung to the hope that I would be forgiven. I had made a mistake and hurt the ones I loved, that was true, but I was my parents' child, I thought, and nothing could change that. Knowing there was nothing my children could do that would make me forsake them forever, I was sure my parents would relent, and that Anca and I would be accepted.

So I found myself with my young daughter in front of my family home, where my mother, father and Ion, the boys' father, waited. Ion was still living there, a year and a half after I'd left, and he continued to do so for a long time afterwards. Now, while Mother took Anca and made herself scarce somewhere in the yard, I sat on the bench under the apple tree in front of the kitchen. I felt that I was under some kind of silent examination. Once again I was feeling out of place, and I breathed a great sigh of relief when Dragos and Carmen appeared. They were young and so full of the positivity of those who are determined to make a good life for themselves that they immediately lifted my spirits.

It was then that I learned that Carmen's parents had been opposed to their marriage. Apparently, they didn't approve of Dragos. But Carmen didn't give up and of course, knowing my son as I did, I knew that she hadn't been wrong in her choice.

That evening her parents came for dinner. They had no qualms about showing me what they thought of me. They didn't talk to me at all, and Carmen's father sat with his back to me the whole evening, as if I was invisible. I found this behaviour incomprehensible. It was the first time I'd encountered such bad manners in guests to our house. But I was even more surprised that my parents didn't seem bothered by it. It was as if they thought this was no more or less than I deserved – to see me humiliated, to make me realise what in their opinion I had lost.

I left the next day, firmly deciding I would never come back and more determined than ever to leave the country.

Back in Mircea cel Bătrân, I thought that the first thing I could do was take a work-related trip outside the country. As it happened, one was being organised, to Czechoslovakia. I applied and was accepted, but, as often happened in those days, just a few hours before departure I was told I couldn't leave. No explanations were given and it would have been futile to ask. I suspected my family had intervened. Then, as misfortune never travels alone, I was informed that my labour contract had been revoked.

"Why?" I asked, bewildered.

"The president told me that he came a few times and he couldn't find you," was the farm supervisor's answer.

This wasn't the real reason, of course. He hadn't liked me from the beginning, due to being compelled to hire me. I told myself that things would be all right, that I would find a solution. In such situations, only someone with a lot of influence could help you out. I remembered a friend of my father's, who was high-up in the Securitate. Like conspirators, we'd referred to him as "Uncle Sandu". I made an appointment to see him in Bucharest.

I am grateful to him for all the good he did over the years when, in critical circumstances, he was always at our side. On this occasion he gave me the name of someone at the county security police. "Tell him I sent you," he said.

It really was like magic, seeing the doors of this fearsome organisation swing open on the mention of Uncle Sandu's name. Two days later, I stood face to face with a most feared individual; the head of the county security police.

"What wind brings you here?" he enquired.

I explained about the difficulty I was having with the local agricultural cooperative leadership. He asked for a few more details, then assured me everything would be fine, and I returned home to Mircea.

The next day a car stopped in front of my gate, and the party secretary for our county stepped out and informed me that I could resume my position at any time. I would be paid for the time I had been at home with Anca, and, as the incumbent farm supervisor had informed the party of his desire to move to another village, his job was available if I wanted it.

I still wanted to have time for the house and Anca. So the supervisor kept his job, I resumed mine, and things carried on as before.

But still the thought of leaving stayed with me. Leaving the country during that period was a risk that threatened your freedom and even your life. Yet, if only we could get to another country, we could make something of ourselves, I thought. Here, among my own, I was alone as if amidst strangers. My parents would never accept me, they would always treat me like a rebel, like a person who had lost her reason, and they would probably keep trying to make whatever life I had more difficult than it already was. We'd be better off far away.

I met Dragos on a train to Mangalia, on the Black Sea coast. It was our first step on a long and unpredictable road. We had arranged to meet someone at a fishing port who could help us leave the country illegally. From the station it was a long way to the fishing docks, but eventually we got a lift to within a few kilometres of the coast. At last we reached a large warehouse, open on the side facing the sea, filled with barrels and tubs, big and small, some full, others waiting to be used. Aside from a few boats tied alongside the wharf, there was nothing else but sand, sun and the endless spread of the sea. We waited, trying to see on the horizon whether the fishermen were on their way home.

When the boats finally arrived at dusk, we found our journey had been a waste of time. The young man in whom we had placed our hopes had fallen in love and no longer had the slightest wish to risk his life on an illegal trip to Turkey.

A week later Dragos, Carmen and I studied a map of Romania's western border. We decided to head for Arad, where Carmen had an aunt and where we hoped to find a possible escape route. We were well received, but Carmen's people were surprised by our intentions. They knew well the risks we would be exposed to. Arad was a border city, and many, many people, especially youngsters, had tried their luck at crossing the frontier. Of course, rumours about what became of them circulated freely. In the evening our hosts invited a few young people from the neighbourhood. The majority of them had one or two escape attempts behind them. We heard some of the most incredible adventures, which had all ultimately been unsuccessful. Some of our guests had got off with just a stiff beating, others had been thrown in jail, and we heard of others who had disappeared altogether.

A few months later, the country was in the throes of events that became known as the 'revolution'. Though we all believed in it, we soon knew it hadn't brought the change the people so desperately hoped for. In the end, nothing had changed, about our country, or our desire to escape it.

After the winter break, all of our group got passports so as to be ready for departure. Dragos was the first to leave. In March, he went to Germany, to our Aunt Valeria. Matei was to meet him there in May and Carmen and I later, in autumn.

In the meantime, however, Matei's parents' health had deteriorated even further. His father had had his remaining leg amputated and could hardly move, so he needed constant supervision. His mother, on a walk one spring morning, had been knocked off her feet by an earthquake. Since then she had stayed in bed. We appealed to the village nurses, but they couldn't come more often than every second or even third day. Their advice was to place his parents in a nursing home; there at least they would receive adequate care.

But Matei couldn't stand the idea of taking them out of their home, and he kept putting it off, hoping for an improvement. Of course that didn't happen. It was hard for him, but it really was inevitable. When finally they moved, we found a friendly community at the nursing home, and then Matei's two aunts moved to live nearby. So at least we knew his parents were being visited every couple of days.

We'd decided Matei would leave first, at the end of May. As the day of his departure drew near, I knew very well the pain in his chest at the thought of leaving his parents. Despite their condition it never crossed our minds that we would not see them again. We were sure that in two years at the most, we would be able to bring them to join us, wherever we might be. It was this thought that allowed us to keep moving ahead with our plan.

On the steps of the railway carriage, Matei's eyes were full of worry. "Am I doing the right thing?" he asked. "Take care of them, please." Then the decisive step was taken, and the train pulled away.

After his departure I was very busy selling the house and furniture. Soon our home seemed deserted, and I no longer felt any sense of belonging. I spent my evenings with Tinca and Toader, who still bravely tried to convince me not to leave.

"It's so difficult, being among strangers. Something will happen here sooner or later; it's much better to be among your own." Even the villagers that knew of our plans urged me to stay. "We're getting along so well," they said.

They were wise and welcome words, that I was grateful to hear. But I was resolute in my decision and didn't feel the slightest urge to back down.

"At least tell us why you want to leave," Auntie Tinca pleaded one evening. It was a chance to unburden my soul.

3

When you make a vow to God, do not delay in paying it;
For he has no use for fools. Whatever you vow, pay!
Better not vow at all than vow and fail to pay.

ECCLESIASTES 5: 4-5

I WAS AT HOME, WITH FAMILY I LOVED AND WHO LOVED ME. I had an excellent job, free time for myself and for my sons, and an enviable material situation.

For almost twenty years I had lived with my husband and our two sons with my parents, in a large house with a large yard. I enjoyed my work and my life. Day after day went by and I never dreamed anything could happen that would seriously disturb our peaceful life. Everything was so clear and settled it was impossible to imagine that it might be otherwise. And yet I also had a sense of foreboding, of something that wasn't right, that would bring about a calamitous change.

"I'm nervous of so much good fortune," I told my family,

whenever they picked up on my unease. As it turned out, my fears were well-founded.

Life had not always been so settled. In 1968, my husband Ion and I had first entertained the idea of leaving Romania.

It came about through Ion's brother, Teodor. Teodor was the oldest of seven children, and was just fifteen when he left for Germany during the war. I didn't know anything else about him other than what I had heard from my sister-in-law, Lola, who used to write to him and who was the only one whom he remembered, as they were close in age. It wasn't easy for her to keep in touch with him because of possible repercussions from the Securitate. If you had the luck to be protected by a high-up connection that wasn't so much of a problem, however. And since my family enjoyed such a privilege, Ion and I decided to meet his brother in Yugoslavia.

Teodor now lived in Norway with his wife and three daughters. He was a mechanical engineer with one of the larger maritime companies, and spent a lot of time at sea. In 1968 his ship was bound for Rijeka and we met him there one evening in August.

During the two weeks his ship was in port we lived with him on board, and there we started to flirt with the idea of leaving with him for Norway. The only things stopping us were the thought that our children were too young to take with us, and the fear that our families might suffer and could lose their jobs. We agreed we would have to find another way. Over the next five years Ion and I managed two visits to Norway. Then, in August 1976, we were able to leave the country in our car, and take the children with us. This time Teodor's ship was headed for Dunkirk, and that's where we agreed to meet him.

I knew my mother would never have been able to accept our departure. She seemed to derive all her happiness from having me and my sister near her. So we didn't tell her, or my father. Instead I left an audiocassette in which Ion and I told of our plans.

We left Romania without incident, drove across Hungary, stayed a night in Vienna, and the next day entered Germany, making for a small place called Hausach. This was where Aunt Valeria lived, and where we would stay until Teodor's arrival in France. Aunt Valeria, as we called her, was my husband's aunt. It was to be the first time he would meet her.

Ion and I had of course been to the West before, but for our boys, this was the first time. Their first reaction was puzzlement. They couldn't understand why there was so much to see in the shop windows, compared with what they were used to. Next came delight and frustration as they loved what they saw, and couldn't have it all.

At the German border a long line of cars had formed, and while waiting I met a few Romanian families that were already established abroad. "You only came to visit?" they asked with a smile. "We wouldn't have thought you'd be all that keen to remain in paradise, now, would you?"

We had to be cautious. The fear that we might have been followed, or that these might be informers, stayed with us, so we changed the subject. Each time we had left the country previously, we had been followed until the last moment before boarding the train.

We arrived at Aunt Valeria's and the days of waiting began. We were not bored, though, because everything around us was so new and beautiful. Then two weeks into our stay, we got a telegram that brought that wonderful time to an end.

"DAD SEVERELY ILL," it read.

From then on my peace was over. I felt guilty for what had happened and didn't leave the telephone for three days and nights, trying to get a connection home. It was surprising that the telegram had arrived okay but now, I was told, the phone didn't work. I knew it must have been tapped but I didn't suspect anything more than that.

On the morning of the fourth day I had the inspiration to call a neighbour. I then found out that my father was in good health and had been all along, and had just returned home from work an hour previously.

We all breathed sighs of relief when I shared the news. Then I heard Aunt Valeria say, "You don't treat your children like this." She could see straight away how my love for my parents was being used against me, but it took me years to fully appreciate how right she was.

Finally, after a month, we got the news that Teodor's ship would be in Dunkirk within the week. We climbed back into our car and drove to Paris, spending what little time we could in this city so full of history, charm and poetry.

We got to Dunkirk late, after midnight, but found it lit up like daylight, full of noise and wildly animated. From the Communist propaganda at home we had heard so much about drugs, prostitution, and other dangers on the other side of the Iron Curtain, that I imagined the worst. I worked myself into such a state I just wanted to hide. We had to find a hotel room, and though I knew a little French, I lacked the courage to start a conversation. In the end it was little Remus who broke the ice, and in a short time we were comfortably settled in a large room with two double beds.

We woke in the morning to the aroma of fresh croissants, and after a delicious breakfast we were ready to go out and explore.

It was two days before Teodor's ship arrived, and once it had, as we did previously, we moved on board with him. We left the car with a friend of his, and in another two days we were at sea en route to Norway. The weather was fine and the days full of activity, so that before we knew it we had reached Narvik, in the north of the country. From there the boys and I were to take the plane to Arendal, where Teodor and his family lived. We were to stay there with his wife Ingrid, while Ion stayed on the ship to work with his brother, until the Norwegian authorities cleared our status.

Ion and I parted company, convinced that we were doing the best thing for our own and our children's future, and that we would succeed.

Everything went according to plan, and the boys and I were met by Ingrid, her sister Eva, and Eva's husband, Johan. When we reached their home, I was glad to recognise the sites Ion and I had visited years previously, when we spent a beautiful winter vacation here. We moved into the house that had been rented for us, a large villa situated not far from our relatives, in a forest by a lake. On the ground floor was a living room, a vast sitting room with white faience fireplaces, gilded armchairs, heavy purple velvet curtains, and wonderful chandeliers, a huge study, a bedroom, a kitchen, and a separate pantry room for the refrigerator/freezer. From the study and sitting room, doors opened into a glazed terrace overlooking the lake, which was surrounded by woods on all sides except in front of the house. The whole place inspired peace, a peace that seemed to come from the depths of the woods and the silent lake. The whole scene enticed you to sit, immerse yourself in it and enjoy it.

Although everything looked perfectly safe, I was still afraid. From the living room, a staircase climbed towards the library, bedrooms, bathrooms and more terraces. The staircase walls were lined with the portraits of family ancestors, whose gazes seemed coldly indifferent to the fear that could be easily read in our eyes in the evenings, as we climbed up to the bedrooms. It was October, darkness fell early, and everything around us felt foreign. We blocked the doors and drew the curtains so that I couldn't see the darkness of the forest, then I would light the fire and sit down with the boys in front of the television, trying to get our ears accustomed to the sounds of the Norwegian language.

During the day, things were easier. When I was not busy in the kitchen we went for walks in the woods around the house, always returning with pleasure to the beautiful front lawn, bordered with imposing, century-old trees stepping down to the lake shore. The beauty and silence of the setting was undeniably moving.

We were free to roam where we liked, and discovered both a small rented house and a comfortable cottage nearby. Eva lived a few minutes away, and every morning when she and Johan took a walk in the woods they would stop for a short visit. Though I didn't speak Norwegian, we understood one another surprisingly well. One morning they brought us some paper bags and urged us to go and fill them with hazelnuts from the forest. They were just waiting to be picked up, they said, and could be sold in the nearby town by anybody who needed the money. We fitted that description, and so we would leave in the mornings, each of us armed with buckets, to search through the long grass for the prized nuts. It didn't take long to train our eyes to the richest places where they seemed to hide.

I didn't say anything to the boys, but my night-time anxiety followed me even here, manifesting as the strange feeling that somebody was behind me. It took me a long while to understand this was simply due to my fear of the unfamiliarity of our surroundings.

Once, the boys went out by themselves, to return only well after dark. Of course I was very worried, but my mood improved when they told me how, despite their growing fears, especially as dusk fell, they were not willing to give up on filling their quota.

They started to call out to each other for the slightest reason, even though they were so close that they could have touched each other.

"Remus, where's the bucket?"

"Look how many there are over here! But where are you, Dragos?"

In one week, picking up and selling hazelnuts earned us over 600 crowns – our first payday abroad.

Our rent was being paid out of Ion's wages, but when I found out how much it was, I asked if there was anywhere smaller and cheaper we could live. A few days later we went to visit a cottage for rent in the mountains. It's okay, I told myself, I love the mountains. But when we got there, I changed my mind. While it had what we needed and the rent was much lower, the cottage was on a mountain peak and there was no one around for kilometres in every direction. How would I get to the shops at the foot of the mountain, I asked, especially if we got snowed in? Ingrid told me that was no problem – I could use skis! I had nothing against that, except that I couldn't ski. And that didn't explain how I would get back up to cottage carrying my shopping bags. At the same time, I didn't think it was right that we should isolate ourselves from people, since we didn't know the language. So, regretfully, I declined, and we stayed where we were.

Often, sometimes daily, the boys and I walked into town, five or six kilometres away. Their favourite store was the music shop. Even when I couldn't come with them, they managed to go in, listen to music, and sometimes even borrow some records from the proprietor, in the hope I would buy one. Although we couldn't afford it, I couldn't turn them down forever, and after a full week of, "Don't Cry For Me, Argentina" everywhere, up and down the house, I gave in.

I now began to wonder what was happening about our immigrant status. The boys were not going to school and I didn't understand what was holding things up. With my limited language skills the subject was too complex for me to discuss, and I could only communicate with Ion through letters that wouldn't reach him until his ship reached a port. So I mainly looked for news from my sister-in-law, who spoke to Teodor regularly by phone. I thought they had gathered the necessary information for immigration before our arrival, but if they hadn't, we probably should have discussed it before deciding Ion would remain on the ship.

I told myself to be patient, and looked for things to do to take advantage of the time I had at my disposal. I had found a Romanian-Norwegian dictionary and tried to decipher as much as I could from newspapers and magazines. It was harder to keep the boys occupied, however, and I wondered about finding them a hobby. One day, when we were in the music shop, I came across a cheap guitar and decided to buy it. I didn't think for a second that this would cause any problems, but when Ingrid next phoned the ship and mentioned what I'd done, Teodor let Ion know how he saw things.

"My children don't have anything like that and yet you, in your circumstances...!" Looking back, I can understand his reaction, but at the time, I had only done what I thought best.

Winter drew near. The three of us stood in front of the window on the top floor of the house, watching the elegant, silent dance of the first snow flakes, which seemed so unnaturally large, before they spread themselves neatly on the ground.

Despite the cold, the boys still spent most of the time outside. They found a boat and took it out on the lake. "We're going fishing," I heard them calling, but I made them come back in. I'd heard the lake was dangerous for the inexperienced, with both very deep waters and hidden rocks that could easily catch novices unawares.

Their next adventure was back in the woods. In the hallway at the back of the house was a stand with pegs on which hung all the keys to the house. The boys had tried them all and discovered one of them opened a storeroom filled with skis, skates, and a couple of chainsaws.

One afternoon it was almost dark, and the boys hadn't returned from the woods. I wasn't afraid any more for them to be out there by themselves, but now they were out later than I expected. Finally, I couldn't bear it, and went out and began calling for them.

Soon after leaving the path, I found myself in snow to above my knees. Then I made out a couple of dark shapes moving among the trees. Certain it could only be them, I called out. It was them, and as they drew nearer, I saw they were wearing skis, pushing a cartful of wood and each was carrying a chainsaw on his back.

Before I had time to exclaim, they were shouting excitedly at me.

"We saw them, we saw the animals!" they called. "Look at the tracks."

"What tracks?" I shrieked, looking around for wolves or bears.

"Don't be scared, mum. They're reindeer. In winter they come close to the houses. Eva told us they come right up to her kitchen window."

Having calmed down, I looked at the cart the boys were pushing. I didn't want to think about the size of tree they'd cut up, or the danger they'd put themselves in by doing it. Right now, they were happy and proud at having contributed something to our housekeeping. I silently decided the best thing to do would be to hide the chainsaws.

We went to Norwegian language lessons a few evenings a week. To save money, we walked there and took the bus back, which dropped us off near the forest, about five hundred metres from the house. With the snow covering everything and gleaming in the moonlight, it was easy to see quite deep into the forest. But we walked quietly, side by side until close to the house, when a race developed between the boys to reach the house first. I would have run as well, but then who would have remained behind to be "eaten"?

We were making steady progress with the language, and I was proud when one day in the food market a salesgirl asked Remus how we were getting along. "Bedre og bedre, dag for dag," he promptly answered. Slowly, slowly, day by day.

Still there was no word about our status. I hardly saw Ingrid, other than when she brought word from Ion on the ship. Neither had I heard anything from home, and I badly wanted to call them. I felt lonely and wished I wasn't, but didn't know what I could do to improve things.

Cecile, the daughter of the house owner, visited from Oslo once in a while. On one occasion, I saw her take a phone from a cupboard and after she'd finished using it, lock it back up. I later found out that Teodor had asked her to keep the phone under lock and key. He'd lived through the same crisis of longing for home and no doubt wanted to protect me by removing the temptation to call. I think it would have been better if he'd explained the danger – it was as if he was treating me like a child. But perhaps he was right. On one of our town visits, we passed the telephone office. I couldn't resist, and handed over the money for an international call. Mother cried so much she couldn't say a word, and I was left feeling distraught I had brought her to such a state. So the call really had made things worse.

Two months passed and we still had not heard anything about gaining residency permits or any kind of official status. Every time I asked Ingrid about it, she couldn't clear anything up. I felt the one person who should have been doing something was Teodor, but he was far away. With nothing to go on, my fear and unease grew. This is a great arrangement, I would say to myself, where nobody lifts a finger to settle us into a normal life. What could I do?

Every evening, I had started to unload my worries onto the pages of a journal. I thought of my mother's sighs, and still seemed to hear them. Why is she doing this? I wondered. Why is she making it harder for me, why is she making herself suffer? I was alive, I was with my children, my husband was working. Why didn't I at least have some support from her? I felt alone and unhappy. Suddenly, I heard myself saying, "God, please help me return home," and then, childishly, "Please help me and I promise to—" Well, let me keep that promise to myself. Let me just say that I was convinced then, and every time I repeated the same thing, that I would carry out what I had promised.

4

It was at this time that Jean came into our lives. Jean was Romanian and had emigrated in similar circumstances and at the same time as Teodor, and the two had remained friends. Like Teodor he had married and lived in Norway, but after his wife's death several years ago, he had remarried a Romanian woman in New Zealand, and settled there.

We'd learned a little about Jean during our first visit to Norway, years previously. During a conversation about a friend of his, Teodor observed that he thought Jean was working with the Securitate in Romania. It was the only way he could explain how his relatives in Romania could leave the country at any time, when ordinary citizens couldn't possibly do such a thing.

That was all in the past now, and Jean had been received as Teodor's friend. So when I learned he was visiting, I asked for his help.

He was a small man, around fifty years old, with a probing look behind his glasses. I took an immediate dislike to him, though I could not have explained why. I simply never felt at ease when he was around. I got the vague impression his true self was hidden behind those glasses. Over the years I've learned that, no matter what the reason, when such a feeling comes over you about someone, it is wise to keep away. At that time, however, as far as I was concerned he was someone who could help me find out something about our situation. I was desperate to know what was to become of us. I was suffering so badly that the idea of returning home had started to take root as a way forward. Here, nobody knew what to do. I was on my own and so was Ion. He should have stayed until we'd clarified what would happen, and only then gone to look for work.

Jean knew well what we wanted. Ingrid had described everything to him in detail and he came across as very well-meaning, especially when he was around me. He expressed real worries about the fate of my family back in Romania if I succeeded in remaining "outside". We'd expected them to have some problems, but Jean seemed very well-informed, down to the smallest details, about what might have happened. Knowing that he often went to Romania and was therefore up-to-date with things there, I didn't have the slightest doubt about the truth of what he was telling us. Neither did we question his good intentions, despite my feelings, because he was Teodor's friend.

For several days in a row Jean, Ingrid and I went to the police station, along with the children, meeting the same officer each time but being unable to understand why we didn't get a result.

Finally, Jean explained the situation.

"The only way to get legal status is to ask for political asylum. But Ion says he doesn't want to do that because of the consequences it would have on your families back home."

So we had to find another way. Perhaps a lawyer could help, I suggested. But nobody else seemed to agree, or come up with any alternatives, so the situation remained unresolved. I wrote Ion a letter expressing my frustration at this impasse, and said either we should go back to Romania if nothing else could be done, or he should come back to the boys and me and together we would find a way to make our status official.

Jean visited daily during this time. He would bring the boys fruits or sweets, then stay to talk about home or about New Zealand, and what a pleasant and quiet place it was.

"Why don't you come there with me?" he asked me one day. I didn't understand quite what he meant, so I told him to talk to Ion and Teodor. He never mentioned it again.

In the meantime, the little house nearby became available, and since the rent was cheaper, we moved in there.

One morning Ingrid came by, a little upset.

"What is it, what's happened?" I asked Ingrid.

She told me that Ion and Teodor were coming home. Though I thought this was good news, I understood that something was amiss and asked if something was wrong.

"Teodor is very upset with you because you wrote to Ion to come home so that you could return to Romania."

I was shocked. "I expressed my opinion," I said, "but if he thought otherwise, he probably would have told me." Ingrid hadn't seen my letter of course, and didn't seem convinced. "Look, if Ion thinks it's wrong to return he doesn't have to come, but he has to tell me."

"Is that what you want?" she asked me.

"Of course," I replied, thinking a phone call would be good enough. In the evening, Ingrid confirmed both men were coming home.

"Why?" I asked. Nobody could or would answer me, but I was to find out the following day.

There was a lot of hustle and bustle at the airport, as anywhere in the world in such places, but once again I couldn't help feeling I was being watched. Embarrassed, I started to look around me, thinking perhaps I was dressed oddly in the winter coat I'd borrowed from Eva. Noticing my agitation, Ingrid asked me what was wrong.

"I can't help feeling people are looking at me."

"I noticed that too," Ingrid said. "But I don't think there's anything wrong. You are very beautiful, that's all."

Under different circumstances such a remark would have gladdened me, but right then I had more to worry about, with thoughts about this sudden return churning through my head. Why is he coming home? Why didn't he write to me? What is going to happen now? What made him take this decision?

When I saw Ion among the passengers it did little to ease my fears. He had lost weight and had a frightened look on his face, as if he was lost somewhere. I became truly worried when he looked towards us. It was as if he couldn't even see us.

Teodor passed me without saying hello, and now it was I who was starting to be frightened. Ingrid came over shortly to try and calm me down.

"It's going to be all right," she whispered.

Once we reached home, I thought, with just us, Ion would be better. But he only said, "I'm too tired now, we'll talk tomorrow." Then he went to bed.

What could have happened, I wondered, if after three months away he comes home and all he can say boils down to just a few words.

The next day he tried to explain, but everything seemed so mixed up that I finally stopped him.

"What made you come home?" I asked.

He looked at me. "I felt I was going to lose my mind, being alone all the time."

Gradually I was able to piece together the picture. Ion hadn't expected the break from us to be so sudden. He'd been surprised by how strongly it had affected him. He'd accepted the job offer thinking he wouldn't be alone on the ship, but it hadn't worked out that way. He seldom saw Teodor when they were at sea, and when they berthed at a port, he would still be alone. Not knowing English he didn't dare go ashore; and if he had done, where could he go? Teodor went, of course. He would leave and return as was typical with any shore leave. Maybe he thought he was helping his brother by leaving him alone among English-speaking people. But when Ion received my letter in which I talked to him about a possible return home, he'd seized on the idea, confessing he had been thinking the same thing. As far as legitimising our status in Norway, all that had been done while he was on the ship had been an attempt to validate his diploma as an electro-mechanical engineer.

Teodor didn't want to see me over the next days. I didn't blame him; he was upset by the failure. "If I had been home, we would have succeeded," was the gist of what he was saying. That may have been true, but it was a bit late for that now. The fact was he hadn't been, and he hadn't done anything else to help his brother either.

Now he wanted to find Ion some work on shore. But it was too late for Ion. "I wouldn't stay here for a pile of gold," he said.

I realised how much he must have suffered, how frightened he had become that he might find himself in a similar situation to that of working on the ship. He simply wasn't able to give our life in a new country one last shot.

We didn't have enough money to return home. So Jean offered to lend us money until the following summer, when he was due back in Romania. Therefore, we agreed to meet him at the train station just before our departure back home. I still found him unsettling, and this was only emphasised by the way he came out

from behind a column at the entrance to the station, immediately
after we had said our goodbyes to Teodor and Ingrid. It was as if he
had been watching us.

So began our return trip. We went back to Dunkirk to pick up
our car and started for home that same night. The boys slept and I
could hardly keep my heavy eyes open, but Ion, as tired as we
were, pleaded with me to keep him company. I started singing to
liven up the atmosphere, a child's song, "Take Me Home, Old
Tramcar".

We stayed for a couple of nights with Aunt Valeria, who was
devastated we'd given up the chance to remain outside. "You won't
get another chance," she morosely told us. I tended to agree with
her. I've never enjoyed going back over the same road, but it just
felt that something stronger than we were was pushing against us,
and we could no longer resist.

We stopped in Budapest to restock, then on an afternoon a few
days before Christmas, reached the Romanian border. Of all of us,
Dragos was the angriest about returning home. But of course it
wasn't up to him.

We arrived at the border at around seven in the evening. Our
inspection lasted until close to midnight. An immigration official
who noted that we were "late" coming back from abroad applied
himself in a zealous check of our details and belongings. I called
my father and Uncle Mircea, who were waiting for us in one of the
hotels in town. Mircea had been the chief of the passport office in
our home county. He had warned us how things would go, and
said now there was nothing to do but keep calm.

Finally we were through and in the morning we started to
cross the country: Oradea, Bucharest, another seventy kilometres
to Oltenița, and home. Around midday we stopped at a cafeteria to
have a snack. As soon as we stepped through the door we were
shocked by the state of the place; the mess, the dirt and the lack of

interest that filled the whole room. These were the aspects of life in Romania we had forgotten. A potato salad that didn't look particularly fresh was displayed in the middle of the food cabinet. There was nothing else on offer.

"What a difference! Where we've been and where we are now!" I heard Remus say behind me.

"What's going on?" I turned to Father.

"Things have changed over the past few months," he explained. "You can find anything you want, but only for a steep price and usually under the counter. We cope all right, don't worry."

"You could at least have told us," I said.

Father simply shrugged. "It's how it is. At least now you're home."

Home. Mother cried, laughed, and sang with happiness to see us back. Relatives, friends, everybody greeted us warmly.

How was I to suspect that once back, my fate, and not only mine, would be caught in the whirlwind of unknown changes? Although, as Father had assured me, we didn't lack anything, it didn't take us long to see that everything had changed for the worse. Overnight, it seemed, the stores had been emptied of most of the prime necessities.

We hadn't left the country too long ago, so we knew the terror people lived under. Now we could feel it for ourselves more keenly than ever. Some time after our return, we were called to the offices of the county Securitate and interrogated separately. The investigators were probably hoping we would be tripped up, but everything went through smoothly. We didn't have much to hide and fortunately, our "straying," as our investigators put it, didn't have grave consequences. After a few more weeks full of unnecessary irritation and stress, and countless influential interventions, Ion and I managed to get our old jobs back.

I thought it was time to keep the secret promise I had made to God, and so I approached Mother, who to my surprise behaved as if she hadn't heard a thing I'd said. I was a little taken aback and was left feeling confused. Had I rushed into making this promise? I asked myself. What if I hadn't taken this decision seriously enough and acted only in a moment of desperation? It was dawning on me that I had acted without fully comprehending the gravity of my decision and that I had launched myself into territory that was still foreign to me. I waited a while, then the days, weeks, and months passed. Although I didn't forget my promise, and I knew there was still something I needed to do, I let myself be dragged along by daily events. In this way, I think, uncertainty and weakness prevailed, the consequences of which were to plague my life for the next twenty years.

5

WITHIN A SHORT TIME, EVERYTHING GOT BACK TO NORMAL. Even the old unease in my soul took up its place again, the anxiety I'd experienced in Norway, of some unknown creature stalking me, changing back into the fear that something less physical but equally terrible was about to happen. One morning I woke from a vivid dream which I was sure had a message for me. I was in a cottage, and without going outside I knew it was somewhere at the end of the world, if such a place existed, on the shore of an ocean. I was sitting on a chair in a corner, holding a girl of five or six years old on my knees. I seemed to be fearful, frightened by something, which made me not want to come out or see anybody. Though I was isolated, I didn't wish it otherwise. Then in the room with us there was an old man who was labouring silently over a simple earthen oven, preparing something for us. I looked at him and said to myself, "It's God who helps us." That was the thought I woke up with.

My job was in the accounts department at the large tobacco packing house run by my father. It was quite common to see soldiers carrying out their drills in the factory compound. They were mainly from a firefighting unit and over time some of the faces became familiar. One day a young officer came in to our office, introduced himself as Lieutenant Matei, and asked for permission to use the phone. As it was his first time in our office, I showed him the arrangements we had in place to protect against fires.

During our little tour, he told me a few things about himself, including that he was single and had arrived in town six months ago from a village in the southern county of Ialomița.

After his departure, the girls in the office told me with one voice, "Madam, be careful. The officer likes you!" Of course I waved off their teasing, but found I was actually quite pleased by the remark. My father appeared shortly after and I gave him the day's report, including Lt Matei's use of the phone. But I didn't mention what the girls had said.

Soldiers from the firefighting unit started to come more and more frequently and the young lieutenant was always with them. On some afternoons he found me alone, and we would chat on the bench in front of the offices. And that was where Ion found us one afternoon when he came to pick me up. He accompanied me back to the office to get my things, where he mentioned it to one of my colleagues.

"I've just found my wife talking with a young lieutenant." His remark was met with a silence that I think all of us found embarrassing, and the dark look on his face didn't escape my notice.

In the car, I asked him directly, "Do you think it was a bad thing that I was talking with that young man?"

"No, of course not," he said, his eyes on the road. "Just be careful. You're someone who isn't well equipped for life in the real world."

"What does that mean?" I asked. I was taken aback, hearing this from my husband, who not long ago had admitted he couldn't be on his own.

"I think you're someone who destroys everything she touches," he said, with a sad smile. *"Une femme fatale."*

A few days later, young Lieutenant Matei showed up just as I was ready to leave for home. He offered to accompany me and I accepted. This happened a number of times after that, with a variety of pretexts. Then we met in town, and he always seemed to find an excuse to drop me off at home. I never turned him down.

I liked my new situation. I felt there was no ulterior motive behind our encounters, and at the same time strongly believed there was nothing wrong with what I was doing. After all, what can happen? If something improper comes up, I will stop. Nobody can force me to do something I don't want.

I told Matei that I was about to start the last section of a three-year course I had been taking in a town about seventy kilometres away. I would be there for a few months. It happened to be where his military command was headquartered, so he would be able to come and see me almost every week, he said.

And so he did. We spent weekends walking, talking, on visits to the confectionery store, telling each other stories, and most of all we laughed. Matei had a great talent for telling funny stories.

One Friday afternoon, just after we had parted company, I was on my way back to my room when I recognised our car. Ion and the boys had come to take me home for the weekend. I realised that I didn't want to leave, and as I sat in the car, unhappy and silent, Ion asked me what was wrong.

"I don't know," I said, not denying it. "But I'm not happy about going home."

The following week Matei waited for me after my course and suggested he take me home by car. Seventy kilometres was not a short trip, but I accepted. We arrived in town, then when he jokingly suggested we turn around and go back I didn't refuse. So we did, just for the joy of being together.

Another day he called and invited me to the military barracks. At the entrance I was greeted by a carpet of lilac flowers; the hallway, staircase and floor all the way to his office were strewn with fresh flowers. In response to my amazement, he said, "They're for you." I was delighted, of course, but now alarm bells were going off in my head loud enough even for me to hear them.

"Thank you," I said, "but I have to go home." Without waiting or explaining further, I left the office. I had to pull myself together, I told myself. I had to stop. With these thoughts I headed home, to find my parents talking about the rumours regarding Matei and me that had started to circulate in town.

"What do you say to that?" asked my father.

Despite my own concerns, I reacted defensively when challenged by my parents.

"I'm not surprised," I said. "What do you expect? It's a small town, we were seen in the street, people love to gossip. It's nothing unusual."

My family were heading off to spend the summer holidays in the mountains. At the last moment we agreed we needed someone to stay at home to look after the place. So, I offered. And every morning at nine o'clock the phone would ring and it was Matei. I almost couldn't wait for the shrill noise that brought me such joy. This went on for about a week until one evening I got an anonymous call from someone wanting to meet me.

She didn't want to give me details over the phone, but said she would wait for me at the corner of our street after dark.

"It is very important," she assured me.

I found a young girl with a beautiful face, who without any formality said, "Listen to me. Please be careful with the phones.

They are tapped and someone is going to try to blackmail you. Tell them everything about Norway or your husband will be told about the fireman lieutenant."

I was stunned, and also very grateful to this girl, who obviously worked for the Securitate, but did not agree with their methods.

It seemed that I was engaged in a fight, and I didn't want to give in. I understood that I needed allies who could help and so I called Vetuţa and Mircea, knowing that through them I could reach Uncle Sandu, who I was certain would help me.

I told Vetuţa everything that had happened.

"Oh, you are in love, what am I going to do with you?" she said, laughing. I told her not to be ridiculous. Then I told myself how impossible this was, and how difficult things were becoming if my phone conversations were going to be tapped. I was determined to take action.

Vetuţa called Bucharest, and to my joy I learnt that Uncle Sandu was going to be in town in a few days. He was the boss of the local security unit, and so, just as I expected, everything turned out all right.

I talked things over with a friend.

"I still don't understand why everyone wants to make a drama out of this," I said. "I never did anything wrong to anyone. And now I need help. I feel that even if I want to I'm not strong enough to give this up. I'm going to tell Ion. I can't lie to him. Surely he'll see that I'm trying to do the right thing and help me?"

"I'm sure he's very handsome," my friend said, "but you have to remember you're playing a dangerous game here. And what do you want? You already have a family, children, a job. What's wrong with all that, why are you so dissatisfied?" She finished with a familiar warning. "Be careful, that's all. I don't think I'm wrong to say you're a person who can destroy everything she touches."

Believing that honesty was the best policy, I told Ion.

"I'm asking for your help," I told him. "What's happening is new to me, it's stronger than I am and I can't cope, I can't fight alone. I need your help."

"What is it?" Ion asked. "What kind of help do you want?"

"I can't give up seeing Matei, and I think going to Germany for a while would be a solution."

As you would expect after such news, Ion was upset. But he told me he would think about it, and I took him at his word.

It didn't take long to find out what kind of thinking he had done. He had asked my parents for advice. They had recommended showing strength, and he agreed. I was now accompanied everywhere I went. I was no longer allowed to touch the phone. And soon Matei was transferred to somewhere in the north of the country. Everybody's attitude towards me changed, and I was treated as if I was completely irresponsible.

I challenged Ion about his response. "I didn't ask for this," I said. "What are you doing? I came to you openly to talk about my feelings, you promised to think about my proposal, and then you act without even discussing things with me. Did you even consider my proposal?"

Neither he nor anybody else would listen to or talk to me.

If this is how they treat me I'm going to leave, I said to myself. I'll decide for myself.

But although I had plenty of good cause to repeat these thoughts to myself day in and day out, I wasn't able to act on them.

I was in the habit of waking early and walking to the gate, where I would look up and down the street, then wander about looking at the flowers, before heading to the kitchen. One morning I found an envelope that had fallen among the flowers by the gate. My heart warmed when I recognised the handwriting. Matei wrote that he couldn't call, that he could only see me from the corner of the street, but that every morning I was to look in the hollow between the fence and the house and I would find a letter there.

Fridays were house cleaning days. One Friday I had just hung the rugs on the wire to be beaten when I heard the phone. After a while I heard Father telling whoever was on the line, "She cannot be with your husband because she is at home." He hung up.

"Who was that?" I asked

"This man of yours is married," he told me. "You must stop it, Elena. It's an illness, I know, a serious illness, but it's not too late."

"Help me leave," I pleaded.

But of course he wouldn't. Nothing I said found an echo in their hearts, or seemed to be of any importance to them. They couldn't keep me locked up all the time, however, and Matei was waiting for me wherever I went, anywhere and anytime he could.

The next time I saw him I asked him about the phone call.

"I had to marry at eighteen," he explained. "I have a son, but we never got along and never will. It's nobody's fault."

"I'm sorry I'm already part of the town gossip, even though I haven't been here long. But any time I say something my wife disapproves of, she runs to the officials. I completely understand if you don't want any more to do with me – none of this is your fault."

I believed him, and told him so. "But you should have told me from the very beginning. Is there anything I can do?"

He took my hands. "Come with me wherever I am sent."

I would have left then and there.

At home, choosing my moments, I again reminded Ion that I hadn't given up on the idea of going abroad. His response was to pretend he didn't hear.

I tried to get closer to my mother, to explain myself.

"I don't want to hear," was all she said, without looking at me, without trying to listen to me.

Then one day, when Remus was in Bucharest preparing for his University Entrance exam, and Dragos was in town, I saw Ion coming towards me. I thought he was heading for the kitchen, when he grabbed my hand and dragged rather than led me along the hall to the bedroom. He locked the door, took out a belt and, still without saying a word, started to hit me.

I cannot hold in pain. I cried desperately under the flurry of blows coming from my husband. I cry now as I write this, as if I still feel the pain and humiliation. The pain took my breath away. I fell to the floor and tried to find a place to crawl so that the belt couldn't reach me, even though I knew there was no such place.

Then my parents came in. Father cried from pity for me but I heard my own mother say, "It's okay, he isn't killing you." Then she gathered up my jewellery. "If you leave, you'll have nothing," she said. I knew then it had been her idea for the beating Ion had given me; it was her idea of a lesson.

"Father, get me out," I screamed against the locked door. But I was trapped until Dragos came home and forced the door open. The next day my face and my body were covered with bruises. I didn't want to leave the house, and face the stares I would get. But my husband and my parents forced me to go to work. Afraid of even more violence, I didn't argue. Nobody at work asked me why I was bruised. They all knew.

A few evenings later Father stormed into the house, furious.

"I went to talk with him and he said he wasn't giving her up. Grab her."

He had visited Matei at his workplace. Ion seized and held me from behind while my mother and my sister pulled the shoes off my feet and the rings off my fingers. "If you leave, you won't have anything," they repeated.

"Why are you doing this?" I finally asked Ion, "Why do you beat me? I believed in you, I came to you to ask for help. Why are you behaving like some common thug?" In response, I got a fist that drove me against the wall. That was so long ago, yet even now, when I pass near a wall I have the vague feeling I will be hit and will try and avoid getting too close to it.

I can't condemn Ion for what he did. He was an angry man, and when you are as sad as he was it is hard to choose the best solution to a problem. He asked for my parents' advice and he was pushed to do what he did. What angered me was that he still asked for their advice when he should have been able to decide for himself. My parents advised him to use force, because they had always been authoritarian with me and I had always responded to force. They knew I couldn't fend for myself when confronted with physical bullying, and that I would do what I was told. They had long experience of not listening to my opinions and of treating me as a child, as someone who needed guidance, since children cannot make their own decisions.

Now nobody was on my side, and although I accepted that I still wanted the chance at least to be heard. But when I heard my sister say to my husband and parents, "Strip her and put her out on the street", when I felt everybody's contemptuous looks and could see that it was always going to be this way, and knowing that with one glass of wine too many Ion would apply the same tough lesson, I knew I had to leave.

And I knew what would come next. I had experienced it before, in the very early days of our marriage. When Remus was only a few months old, Ion had come home from a meeting with his sister in Bucharest and told me he wanted a divorce. We had never had serious clashes of opinion; it didn't cross my mind that he might not love me or that there might be another woman involved. I married at nineteen and such thoughts were alien to me. I struggled to understand things that I felt I should have known, such as what the birth of a child meant. It wasn't just the innocence of a young girl. My mother had avoided discussing "such things" with me, and I understood that after the wedding Ion blamed her for my ignorance. All I knew was that you had to be faithful to your husband and that you had to work for the good of the household. These things were true in themselves, but not sufficient to make a marriage work.

So I didn't understand what was going on. "Why do you want to leave?" I begged. "What have I done wrong?" He wouldn't say anything other than that he wanted to leave. What should I do? I asked myself. Where has this evil come from? Whom should I turn to, whom should I talk to about it, whom should I ask, what can I do?

The day after Ion told me he wanted to leave, my parents were to go abroad. I was sure that this news would have stopped them, and because I didn't want to upset them, I didn't tell them. I just kept asking Ion, why? Why did he want to leave us? I was crying, pleading for explanations. I had the right to one, I tried to argue. For the sake of the child, I said. Then I found myself on my knees begging him not to go.

In the end, he relented. I'd persuaded him to stay, to give us another chance. The years went by, we had another boy, the children grew up, we got along well. Occasionally we had arguments, like any couple, but with good will on both sides they always ended well. We were admired and respected by everyone that knew us.

Now I had told him the truth about my situation. I had asked him to help me, and he beat me. That was what I couldn't understand. When he had said he wanted to leave, I had pleaded with tears, with kindness. Now, when I was the one wanting to go, he never once asked me to reconsider, to stay.

When I married I stepped out into life without knowing what I was doing, and without anybody guiding me. Knowing this, Ion was afraid I would give in to temptations at every turn. I could see now that this fear was behind his incomprehensible fits of jealous rage.

If I didn't act now I would regret it, I thought. Come what may, it would be better to leave than to carry that regret and fear for the rest of my life.

Matei had been transferred to the north, and from there he called every day hoping to reach me, although this happened very rarely. His divorce had been finalised a little before his transfer. He wanted me to go to him there, but it wasn't that easy. Though I thought about it all the time, I couldn't take the decisive step.

I had gone to bed early when I was woken by a noise outside. My father burst like thunder into our bedroom.

"He was here! He came here, into our yard, I found him here, do you understand?" He was addressing Ion. Although it must have been obvious that I hadn't the slightest idea what was going on, nobody wanted to listen to me. Instead I had to sit while they threw their accusations at me, content at least that they didn't apply the usual lesson.

The next day I found a letter waiting for me. Father must have surprised Matei in the act, but not knowing what he was doing, had not searched the area closely. In his letter, Matei said he had flown in from the north of the country to wish me a happy birthday, to come and be close to me. He insisted I should go to him there.

I didn't expect peace and quiet in the house, but those days were increasingly hard to bear. I tried to endure the pain for the children's sake, but I couldn't. They were mine, I loved them and they loved me and that's why I didn't expect to be hurt, to be treated with contempt by those who should have loved me. I would have liked to see their goodness, understanding and love. Maybe it was too much to ask, seeing as I was the one who had brought about this mess. But even so, I couldn't live this way. As I write, the old suffering is stirred up, suffering I wanted forgotten and that makes my soul writhe in pain. Why did this happen? I was a peaceful person, devoted to my family, a person who loved calm. Why did I have to be cast into the heart of a storm I couldn't withstand? I didn't know anything about situations like this, other than perhaps from books or films, but there is a difference between looking at them and dealing with them. What had pushed me onto this unknown and difficult path? How was it that, while fully aware that fate had been generous to me, I gave up everything, driven by desire? I had let myself be drawn into the pleasure of the play. I needed help and didn't get it, and instead was pushed unwillingly onto a path I would never have chosen. I felt as you feel when you act against your nature – I was unhappy. You do something bad when you don't know better. My conscience had told me what I was doing wasn't right, but still, didn't what had happened since then prove otherwise?

Finally, I acted. Costin, the lawyer who had helped Matei with his divorce and who was also a friend, came by one evening. I put a few things in his car and we left for Bucharest. His wife, Florentina, a pretty young woman, met us. Seeing my agitation she stayed by my side for the best part of the night, while I talked non-stop.

Matei was going to meet me the next morning and together we were to return home, but before his arrival I phoned and arranged to meet Ion at Mircea and Vetuţa's place. How much I would have liked to hear him say, "Come back, I can't live without you," or any words that showed he had feelings for me. Instead he did nothing but offend me, using words I didn't think he was capable of using, as if that was what I needed to hear. I left the apartment to meet Matei.

We went to Fălticeni, where he now lived. We found a nice

apartment near his military unit. Then I turned round and said I was going home, to see my children, and left.

They were all at home except the boys. Mother and Father retreated to their room, and through a window looked on at the fight that ensued immediately between me and Ion. They were like an audience waiting for a show to start. They weren't disappointed. I couldn't defend myself from his blows; when I escaped from him, all I could do was leave.

A week later I was back. The whole scene repeated itself. I still didn't get to see my sons, and my parents looked on as my husband beat me. Then they watched me leave, still through the window, their eyes full of reproach when I said I would never come back.

I did come back, two and a half years later, with Anca. But it was no longer my home, where I had lived a comfortable life without a care in the world. I felt humiliated by their looks that seemed to say, "You are no longer the person you were." I regretted having returned. But at least they didn't beat me.

We stayed in Fălticeni for only a few months. Thanks to my family, Matei was given a disciplinary transfer to another town. There had been an uproar regarding his being divorced, and in their anger my parents had contacted the most influential people they could in the leadership of the Fire Command. This led to his personnel file being stamped "disciplinary," which was going to bring nothing but trouble. So we had to give up the idea of settling down there. And so we ended up on a bus to the Bărăgan.

6

AUNTIE TINCA AND UNCLE TOADER HAD LISTENED TO MY story in silence.

"Now," I went on, "I want to leave. My parents will never accept me. The Ion I know will never leave them. If I stay, we'll only end up in a silent struggle, which he will win. I know my father is the one shouldering the boys' expenses, but by putting on a caring face for them, Ion will stay in the house. I am leaving with Dragos and Carmen. It will be another five years till Remus can follow us, and in the meantime, somehow, we'll get by."

These were my thoughts as I was about to leave my homeland, without any real idea of where we would go or what we would do.

Matei sent gifts and letters from Paris, painting life there in bold colours. Though I knew how he could gloss over things, and how easily he became enthusiastic, I believed him. I wanted things to be the way he said they were and couldn't bear the thought it might not work out as well as we hoped. I relished the treats, and pictured him in a job, and saw myself already living in France. What more could I wish for? I couldn't wait to leave.

Matei's parents by now were accustomed to their new residence, and the only thing that worried them was that we would be so far away, "Will we ever see each other again?" they asked. "Will we live to see Anca growing up?" Of course, these were entirely understandable questions in the circumstances, which it was not possible to answer other than with hope.

Our house and furniture sold, I finally obtained my visa, and one by one I worked through the countless tasks involved in moving out for good. My father and Remus came to collect the grain and poultry. I was proud of myself for being able to give them something I'd grown through my own hard work. I had over a hundred poultry birds, fifty baskets of corn and thirty sacks of wheat.

Remus was supportive, agreeing that leaving was the right thing to do. Father was more reserved, of course. And again, that was understandable.

I left Mircea cel Bătrân village in the summer of 1990. I had felt at home in this little village populated mostly by elderly people. Maybe it was because I loved their customs, the way they talked and the way they lived. Perhaps it was the traditions they observed. I felt my true country was here and nowhere else. I had lived in this simple, calm environment for four years. Nearly three years of hard work had built us a home where I had given birth to Anca, where we had gained people's respect and even won their hearts. Now I was leaving everything we'd built for the unknown.

With everything sold, I spent a few weeks with one of my relatives in a town about fifty kilometres away, then on the morning of August 21 arrived at the station, ready to board the train for Paris. Carmen – Dragos's wife – had left by plane a few days before me.

In Bucharest I was seen off by my relative, a friend and Remus's Carmen. Remus could not come as he had exams that morning. Carmen was wearing one of the dresses I had given her; they no longer fit me well, but were all very pretty, so I had given them to her.

"I will always think of the person who wore them before me," she said.

The train was delayed three hours, and nobody could wait that long. Carmen handed me a letter that she asked me to read after the train left, and took out a specially prepared white handkerchief. "I wanted to wave it when you left," she laughed.

We hugged, and they left, then Anca and I found our seats. I arranged our luggage and a little nest for Anca, and when the train pulled out, I impatiently opened Carmen's letter.

Bucharest, 16 August, 1990

These lines are not addressed so much to Remus's mother, as to the woman I would have loved and prized as much regardless of the place or time I met her. I am writing to a woman who fascinates me, a delicate character, a fighter, sincere and rational but also childlike, impetuous and melancholic, like a character only a master writer could create.

Those days in Reviga are unforgettable. We were a family despite the prejudice: we ate, we drank, we made plans together like some well-heeled family in a classic novel. We talked politics, we criticised the party, we didn't hide our feelings for one another. Truly, those were great days!

I have such wonderful memories of you. I don't have a blood relative like you, but I feel as if we are kin; I just feel better when you're around, and I can express my thoughts and feelings openly. I feel like we're from the same time, the same age. I love you!

Though I've only known you for such a short time, you're

like a legend to me. A mother, a lover, a rebel, a friend, a humanitarian, a myth that wasn't just introduced to me by Remus, but who already existed in my psyche as a feminine ideal. I see myself in one of your gestures, your words, your agitation, your energy, your fight against inertia.

Don't forget me when you arrive!

My blood curdles when I hear I have to leave for somewhere far from the country I know. It whispers to me to be wary, to ponder, to probe. I fear for you as well. But have courage, strength and hope. You are still young. You have beside you an able and courageous man, and a child for whom you deeply wish to do the right thing, to raise her well.

Whenever I think of 'there', I become emotional. Maybe when I am your age I will have more courage. When you get 'there,' you'll have a lot to do. I don't believe in childish dreams of easy money. The most important thing is to keep healthy and keep your mind awake. If you have some free time, write me a few lines. I am not looking for literature, just anything that I know you've written.

And most of all, when you get 'there,' don't fall into the trap of nostalgia. Remember both the good and the bad. Don't try and put an equals sign against your past, don't make concessions just because of the distance. And most of all, remember Remus as often as you can, this superb child who didn't benefit from your presence, who won't have you around at a critical time of his life. Don't get me wrong – I'm not reproaching you. I'm saying these things because I know who I am writing to, and I know that your pain is excruciating. I'm not judging. We've talked a lot about this, and I also understand what has not been said in words, that your suffering remains.

So, this is conjecture. Maybe one day Remus will be with you again. I know he loves you immensely; he loves you like no one else. When I met him, three years ago, he said that his mother was not alive, that she had died. Now you are leaving. Don't die – this is essential for him. Don't treat this matter with tears but with wisdom.

You are strong and so I know you won't think my letter has taken an unduly depressing turn. It's just as if we were talking, the two of us. Stay the same! Don't spoil Anca. A middle road has to be chosen, 'neither breaking, nor spoiling', to quote Camus. And to Mr. Matei, the same: I hope he doesn't change his temperament or his extraordinary spirit, that he stays the same 'give-them-hell' man, who, as we say, 'makes a whip out of shit.' Stay together to stay strong! Yours is a winning combination and it mustn't change.

I wanted to gather my thoughts, to extract the essence from the heap of impressions I have about you. I don't know how much I have managed to capture but anyhow, one thing is certain: 'man can make a place holy.' All hopes can be fulfilled, at least partially. What it comes down to is to have strength in your body and your thoughts, be healthy and keep a clear mind.

I wait to hear from you. But my impressions won't change. You cannot disappoint me. One can only allow oneself the luxury of being honest with very few people in one's life.

Kisses! Good luck! Carmen.

I read that wonderful letter several times on what seemed an endless trip. Each change was difficult, with the weight of our luggage and Anca's small hand. In Prague, the platforms seemed miles apart, but there were kind-hearted people to help. The train was packed, and everyone seemed in such a hurry to get away, to escape the burden of Communism. The fear that maybe it could return one way or another made people swarm everywhere.

The last fifty kilometres to Paris seemed to take an eternity.

But at last I could dream about the new life ahead of us – and it was wonderful!

At Gare de l'Est, Matei, Dragos and Carmen were all waiting for us. Anca threw herself into her father's arms.

I recalled an evening after Matei had left when Anca and I were coming back from the village. In the distance we saw a man on a bicycle going through the gate to our house.

"Look, Daddy is here!" Anca cried.

She was so convinced I almost believed it myself. It was the postman; but at least he was bringing a letter from our daughter's much-loved father. And as I watched her hug him now, I remembered the phone call we'd received at my relative's place, and Anca picking up the receiver. "Daddy, it's Daddy," she danced about, shouting, and big tears rolled down her cheeks.

Now, finally, she was by his side and she couldn't care less about anybody else. We were all talking flat out, wanting to share everything, then and there. The crowd carried us along to the exit, to the subway, and somehow we ended up in front of a hotel. Matei and I were to stay here. Dragos and Carmen were camping in a tent in the Bois de Boulogne.

What would have happened, I wonder sometimes, what course would our lives have taken, if at that time, in that hotel room, I had learned what the future held for us? I was confident, fearless, even, as I looked ahead full of hope and belief. I believed in our youth, in our resourcefulness, and in my own ability to adapt to anything. I still believe that the power of adaptability helps you to survive. I had that truth proved to me many times over in the years that followed. But at that time we didn't have the slightest idea what it meant to leave your own country in the hope of finding residence in another. We had no idea what we needed to do. But we would get to know.

7

THAT NIGHT, WHILE MATEI AND I TOOK ANCA TO FIND something to eat, Dragos and Carmen went to the hospital across the street.

They were visiting a friend of theirs, Mrs. Mihailescu. Mrs. Mihailescu had come from Romania a year earlier with her nine-year-old daughter, and checked into the hospital. Her daughter had brain cancer. She had helped Dragos and Carmen with a lot of what they needed to know as new refugees. An engineer by training, she had no qualms about cleaning, ironing or cooking for work, though she had learned that her employers were often embarrassed about it.

"When you look for work," she later told me, "don't tell them your background. It will be easier for you." It was good advice.

Meanwhile, I found out that Matei had paid for the hotel room with the last of his money, but only for that night. He had hoped I would bring more money from home, but I had left most of what we had with his parents. And so, when I had to pay for the food, the questions started. First off was, "what are we going to do from tomorrow night?"

Dragos and Carmen re-joined us and as we ate I tried to find something out about their situation and what they'd learned in the past few months regarding our chances of obtaining residency in France. They were not optimistic. I was slowly accepting that the road ahead of us would be long and not easy.

I woke early the next morning, as usual. On the balcony I felt the soft breeze chasing golden leaves along the sidewalks. People were rushing here and there, merchants were putting fruit and vegetables, fish, sweets and meats outside their shops. On top of everything the aroma of warm bread drifted by. It was all so tempting. At lunchtime Anca and I each got a huge sandwich that seemed like a horn of plenty. The whole place seemed a natural wonder to us.

Matei and I, loaded with suitcases, bags and satchels, headed for the charity organisation, Secure Catholique. Here we met Monsieur To, a little man who stroked his beard and studied us with kind and lively eyes while he listened to us. He agreed to pay for a hotel room for us, for a period of three weeks. It was modest – a double bed, a wardrobe, a table with two chairs and a sink – in a building near Gare de l'Est, but we were very glad to have a secure roof over our heads.

Dragos and Carmen visited us daily, and on the weekends they stayed overnight. I bought a small gas ring and cooked food we bought from the Ed grocery store. We called it, "the poor people's store," though to us it was a store full of riches. We started to explore Paris with a view to having our status there legalised. That meant getting the famous yellow cards – identification cards that gave you the right to work. We left in the morning and returned in the evening dead tired. We met refugees everywhere; some of them were doing all right, others were looking for work, still others were thinking of moving on, to more distant countries such as Australia. Matei still saw everything in glowing colours. He thought of himself as a lucky man, and was sure we were going to be fine. For my part, I began to think that it would be hard to fend for myself in a world I knew nothing about.

Once you had your yellow card, the next struggle was for a place in what they called the "foyer," a multi-storeyed hostel where immigrants seeking residency were processed. And so we began an almost daily commute between the hotel and France Terre d'Asil. Every time we went, we waited hours in a very large room, trying to get an interview with one of the clerks. It was chaos, with people of all nationalities trying to get their permits. And though it seemed like some people were making progress, day after day we were met with the polite and formal, "Je suis désolée," said with a smile that somehow seemed so cold and indifferent.

Dragos and Carmen were assigned to a kind young man who offered them a place in the hostel at Châteaudun. Matei was still unconcerned, apparently thinking that Monsieur To would take care of us till the end of time. I was upset; I didn't want to have to part from Dragos and Carmen. After meeting and liking them, the "foyer" director in Châteaudun offered to give us a room as well, but he needed approval from the central office. Knowing what was waiting for us we reluctantly went back, trying at first to talk with a female clerk. "Come back tomorrow," she said over her shoulder. Finally, crying with anger, I went to the office manager. In my appalling French, made worse by the state of frustration I was in, I eventually got across why I was there. The clerk was called in, but even though we had all the paperwork in place, nothing was resolved.

While all this was going on I met and befriended Mrs. Mihailescu. She was a brave woman, hoping and fighting for a miracle in the face of her daughter's fate. A year had passed since she had checked into the hospital; she had learned the language, she knew many people who helped her and in turn she wanted to help me. She started by recommending me to some ladies that needed help; for one I ironed, for another I cleaned a small apartment that already shone with cleanliness. It wasn't much, but enough for food. One morning I woke up worrying that we had no money, but then I remembered that today was a working day. What a joy it was for all of us when that afternoon we counted the 170 francs I'd been paid!

I liked the short bus trip I made twice a week to my cleaning jobs. I have always liked studying people's faces, trying to see what lies beyond a smooth face or wrinkles. I used to look at each line and try to decipher there some aspect of life, what was hidden behind a smile or a frowning forehead, to find a truthfully lived life. I didn't like women with smooth faces and no wrinkles, although I would try to estimate their age by the look of their eyes. They didn't say anything, those smooth *visages*; all I could see was a boring life.

Dragos was the first to find real work, as a gardener. A council car would drop him and some others off at one of the many gardens and green areas in the city, then pick them up in the afternoon. He did that for three weeks before he found a job as a courier driver. He'd neglected to mention that he had never driven a commercial vehicle before, but he and the van managed to survive the first week. Along with the money we were given by the government, we were not complaining.

Next, Matei found work at a watch assembly plant. It was good money and easy work, but it didn't last long. Matei found it hard for him to bear the thought that, having once had people working under him, he now had to take orders and work alongside day labourers. His hurt pride made him boastful, and he would talk about how he soon would find something better than this. His words were passed on and in less than three weeks he was fired. I was angry; we had chosen this situation so we had to put up with the consequences. On top of that, despite our circumstances, he would buy wine every night. I felt hurt at the money being spent on something I didn't consider absolutely necessary, but I knew this was a subject on which we would never agree.

We visited Monsieur To every time we needed to extend the term of our stay in the hotel. I still remember with gratitude this warm, humane man who was so helpful. On fine mornings I would take Anca to the playground at the nearby park, and on weekends all of us would go into the city. Years ago, on our first failed emigration to Norway, we'd had time for just a hurried glance at Paris. This time, we could explore its little streets and hidden corners, and pause to feel the mystery that seemed to coat the solid walls of its old buildings. We knew we couldn't stay too long in any one place, and we didn't want to miss any opportunity to visit sites about which we had read or learned, or seen in movies, that stood witness to so much of history.

We visited Notre-Dame cathedral, that monumental construction whose deep shadows, great arches and dizzyingly high ceiling evoked in me the feeling I had entered an unreal world. In the Luxembourg Gardens we discovered a beautiful playground, but you couldn't get in unless you paid. We couldn't afford it, so I looked the other way when Matei and Dragos lifted Anca over the fence. She had a lovely time by herself, even if it was only for a short while.

On the day when entry to the Louvre was free, we joined a seemingly endless line of people who had the same idea. When inside at last, I shivered with joy at the beauty there, despite the crowds. There seemed to be something in the paintings about life in past eras, about secrets that were meant to stay buried, that gave me some insight into my own times.

Our transport bill would have been enormous if not for the Metro, where, we soon learned, you could travel without a ticket. A huge web spreading beneath the big city, the Metro was a subterranean world without sunlight or flowers, along whose meandering paths its people thronged, freed from the authority of trams, buses or cars. From one end to the other of the long corridors we heard wonderful voices give life to immortal operatic arias. We heard suffering and joy vibrate on the strings of violins and cellos, and saw painters showing their work to wave after wave of people squeezing along the corridors. With the little money we had, but with all of our hearts, we contributed whatever we could to those artists who touched us, making us forget even if for just a few minutes how uncertain our lives were. And whenever the airs reminded me of my homeland, I would stop to listen and let my tears flow freely.

The five of us were always together on Friday nights, and we would gather around the phone booth at the street corner near our hotel to get some news from home. One midnight when it was easier to get a phone connection, I met two men coming out of the park across the street. They were Romanians, and they confessed that for two weeks they had slept in the park on benches. I would have liked to take them upstairs to our room so that they could at least wash their feet, but the hotel owner stopped me. "I let your son come and stay, even though it's not permitted. But please, no strangers," he said.

Instead I took them a few bottles of warm water and something to eat, and we shared the few things we had learned in our time as refugees.

One weekend we visited the Clignancourt and Montreuil fairs. Although the animated life of fair goers and visitors reminded me very much of our own fairs, this was a whole new experience. There seemed to be no end to them, and it was so easy to get lost in the multitude of people. But of course at the core of this unimaginable hubbub was the same old question: "How much?" There were so many tempting items, especially with autumn approaching and we with very little to wear. I had packed my beautiful fur coat, but it didn't seem to fit our new lifestyle and I had tried to sell it.

Our favourite place was Barbès, a produce market that stretched the entire length of a street every Wednesday and Saturday. It was so tempting – fruits, vegetables, meat and processed meats, cheeses, sweets, fish and anything else you wanted. The sights and sounds and smells were a feast for the senses. We could buy a little fruit, but got just as much pleasure from admiring the diversity of food, sniffing the aromas of herbs and flowers and soaking in the tumult of market life. As the market broke up, we would head home, usually with a diversion into the famous Tati department store. Matei stayed outside with Anca while I squeezed in to yet another crowd. But where the outdoor markets literally shouted colour and diversity, inside everything silently screamed abundance and wealth. Often Matei would say, "The French should go to Napoleon's tomb every day and kiss it with thanks." All kinds of clothes and accessories lay in heaps as if somebody had just come with full baskets and overturned them onto the counters. To be in the midst of so much, and unable to afford even the most insignificant thing, was a kind of suffering. Outside again, I would remind myself that those things were not for us – now. Then I would put it out of my mind, until my next confrontation with such conspicuous luxury that seemed to be everywhere you turned.

One Friday evening Dragos surprised us by turning up alone.

"Where's Carmen?" I asked. I was trying to make a bed on the floor with everything warm that we had. I took one look at him, then signalled to Matei, "Let's go."

"Mum, what are you doing...?" Dragos tried to stop me.

But I didn't want to listen. I knew they had had a fight, and was sure that as in most cases, stubbornness had replaced reason. I didn't want her to be left alone.

We took a taxi to the Bois de Boulogne, and there I found Carmen crouching in a corner. She was scared, of course, which didn't surprise me. Their tent was set up outside the main camping area with just one other tent beside it and then nothing but the dark night.

On our way back I was a little more relaxed. I would have liked to see more of the nightlife that went on under the beautiful lights of the city, but like any city, this one had a hidden side, one that wasn't so well lit and that scared me. I preferred the simplicity of our routine: waking at dawn, feeding the birds and the animals, going about our daily activities of children, minor worries, reading, discussing current events. These things don't torment your soul, cause great pain, or make you fearful.

Then I noticed on the side of the road, half hidden in the woods and turning away from the bright lights, women in loud make-up, dressed as if for the stage. "It's their time of the night," Matei explained to me. Sensing my shock, the taxi driver couldn't resist chipping in. "The most beautiful ones you see are in fact men," he said.

I was speechless; I just wanted to return as quickly as possible to the small hotel room that represented my home, my safety. I had the feeling of an honest person who thinks himself a sinner just by being near sin. I knew there were bad things in the world, but I didn't want to hear about them, much less come into contact with them. They weighed on my soul.

Back in our room, I finished arranging the bed on the floor, while Matei lightened up the atmosphere.

"I've forgotten how a bed feels since I left home," he joked.

"I've been sleeping on the floor for so long that my back is calloused. If I had only known!"

When I left home my cousin had given me the New Testament and Psalms, with the instruction to read Psalm 51 as a dedication. I hadn't started to read the book, but I did keep it under my pillow, which made me feel safe. A good number of years passed before I finally read it – "Have mercy on me, O God, according to your unfailing love" – and understood its significance.

We had a five or six month wait before our application for residency would be heard in court, and in the meantime we had to provide for ourselves. The biggest problem was accommodation. The churches were always giving away packages of food, and very occasionally we managed to get food tickets for a restaurant, but finding a place to live was trickier.

The restaurant tickets were a real treat; one we went to was on the Champs Elysées, one of the most famous, and expensive, streets in the world. We hardly ever came here, except to change buses or trains. On this long straight road, thick with cars and people, I tried to avoid gazing in the shop windows so filled with luxury and elegance. But of course we were surrounded by it in the restaurant, from the waiting area at the entrance through to the range of food, how it was presented, and the class of the waiters and diners. I hadn't expected such a stark demonstration of the gap between our lives and those who lived in this world, and I had to pretend not to notice the curious glances we were getting from others. When it came time to choose something, I had no idea of what I was ordering. So I picked something at random, hoping only that it would turn out to be some treat I couldn't possibly have prepared in our hotel room.

Shortly before Dragos and Carmen were to move to Châteaudun, they stayed in a transit hostel, in a suburb a long way from ours. Now it was our turn to go to their place on Fridays. At the end of the week they could offer us a free meal in the hostel cafeteria. But the food wasn't particularly good and, on top of that, I was unhappy that we were apart. I always thought our best chance for success was to stick together. We had left together, we had to stay together.

Back at our hotel, another young couple from Romania moved in. Cristi and Melania had married a year previously, while still students at Bucharest University. They'd left everything behind to come to the West. Melania was a beautiful, gentle, patient and very wise young woman. Cristi was handsome and quick-witted, although I did think he was a bit of a dreamer. His father lived in Austria, and they had initially made for Vienna, hoping for some help from him. But none was forthcoming, so they decided to try their luck in France. Being without travel documents, they had hidden in the roof of the train, and were still complaining of back pains when they moved into the hotel. Melania, Cristi and I spent time together every day. When Matei was working or was looking for work, I was glad to have somebody with me as I went to the usual places: Barbès, the churches, the markets. In the evenings they would come to our room and talk till late. Cristi loved the work of the expatriate writer Panait Istrati, and we would discuss his life and thoughts, along with other exponents of our art and culture who had lived in Paris, and who had shared our intellectual values.

We were all fighting to survive. One day in the subway a gypsy got on the train, and, holding himself up at the front of the carriage, shouted out, "Je suis de la Roumanie". Then he started limping down the carriage, obviously to elicit pity. I followed him with my eyes when he got off and of course he began walking perfectly normally. I felt ashamed. Such people didn't represent Romanians. I had nothing in common with them, even if we did speak the same language and had lived in our beautiful land. I have always had a clear voice, and often spoke a little too loudly. At home, one of my girlfriends used to say, "I came to hear your little bell," or, "I heard your little bell from out in the street." After that episode on the subway, I told myself I should be more careful with my little bell.

But I often slipped back to my normal volume, and so I wasn't surprised when, as I was getting off the subway with Cristi and Melania, a man stopped us and introduced himself. Jura spoke Romanian with a strong accent, a result of having left the country many years ago. We exchanged information, without hiding our situation from him, and he immediately offered to help. He was an architect, he said, with a team of workers, and there was always room for someone extra to push a wheelbarrow. He paid three hundred francs a day. Cristi took up his offer.

8

———

SOMETIMES WHEN WE WERE ALONE MATEI WOULD FILL ME IN on what had happened when he and Dragos had first left Romania. It was Matei's first time outside the country and even in Czechoslovakia he was shocked by what he saw. It was still a communist country, but everything was done differently and so much better, incomparably better, than in our own country. Why had a country as rich as ours, with such talented and hardworking people, been left behind? It was disgusting, he said.

"Now I understand why they wouldn't let us leave." He felt we had been wronged, and that nothing would change in Romania anytime soon.

Germany had seemed to him like a construction model that you could only touch gingerly lest you disturb its perfect whole. He met Dragos at Aunt Valeria's, and after a few days they left for Paris, full of hope for the future. Aunt Valeria accompanied them to Strasbourg, from where they hitch-hiked, in seven different cars, to their final destination. People were very understanding and one of them even offered the two men some pocket money. They slept in subway stations, hiding to avoid the pre-closing inspections then setting up a place to sleep. They had a salami from Germany and Dragos would cut them just two slices apiece each night.

They travelled without train tickets, but they weren't always lucky enough to escape without being checked. Most subway stations had more or less the same system, the same way to get to the platforms. But there were always exceptions, and some newer systems were more sophisticated, making it much more difficult to get past without a ticket. Whenever they encountered something like that, they took time to study the terrain. Once, after Matei had passed through the barrier, he looked back to see Dragos with his head caught as if in a vice by the gates. Dragos couldn't talk, his face was lobster-red and Matei could only see the blue of his eyes, bluer than ever now, pleading for help. Beside himself with laughter, Matei quickly called one of the station personnel. Dragos had tailed the person in front of him as they were passing through the barrier, but got his timing wrong and only his head had made it through.

On another occasion Dragos was late to meet Matei at their agreed place. Finally Matei caught sight of him behind a large window, again desperately signalling for help. It took a while to find someone to unlock the room and then find out what had happened. Dragos had seen a subway worker go through a door he was certain would take him past the barriers, and had followed her. Unfortunately, she climbed some stairs, the door locked behind him and Dragos was stuck.

For a month, they didn't have a safe place to sleep. One night, they went to a police station to try their luck. They were sent to an address with the assurance they would be accepted. They got there after midnight, after all the lights were out, but were admitted, given pyjamas, and sent to the bathroom. They came out, found a mattress and then fell asleep, dead tired. At seven in the morning they were woken for a roll call, and fell in line behind all the other men. Finally, they had a chance to look around more carefully. The great majority of the inhabitants were elderly, and all of them had physical defects. One lacked an arm, another an eye, another moved very slowly due to an oozing wound on his leg. One of the staff approached Matei and Dragos and asked what they were doing there.

"Whoever sent you made a mistake," he said. "These are vagrants, the beggars of Paris. In the morning we drop them off around the city and at night we round them up and bring them back here."

I had seen these people myself now, their presence as much a part of the Parisian scenery as those luxury goods stores.

For a week Matei and Dragos slept in a Trabant car, borrowed from a Romanian they met at the French Red Cross. The Red Cross was where everyone who had left home in search of a new life used to meet and receive any mail.

Finally, fortune smiled on them. In one of the many queues that refugees and immigrants find themselves, they met the "penitent gypsy". This man, from Romania, was well known in the community of Paris gypsies as a pickpocket and shoplifter. After many years of a not exactly Christian life, he had turned over a new leaf, and from then on lived a modest but honest life.

The penitent gypsy took Matei and Dragos to the Kopen family, who lived in a large, roomy villa in the suburbs. The house was being renovated, and its owners, Andrei and Tina, were both Romanian gypsies who had lived in France for more than fifteen years. They lived with their four children, and Tina's mother. Tina was a good-looking brunette of around forty. She didn't often laugh, but was always extremely calm, elegant and, most of all, she had a heart of gold. It was she who helped us get our work permits, which needed an invitation from a French citizen, and she obliged.

Now, she looked Matei and Dragos up and down and said, "You seem to be educated people. We're gypsies but if you want to stay, stay, you are welcome. We need help, we don't stay home very much, so try to be as useful as you can." I met her later. I remember her now sitting at the head of the table, making decisions with a cup of coffee in front of her and a cigarette in her hand.

Dragos and Matei stayed with the Kopens until a little before Anca and I arrived. They were alone in the house most of the time because everybody else was out, returning only late at night. The Kopens owned a store near the subway entrance, they said, so it was not surprising they weren't home much. One day, when Matei and Dragos were working in the yard, the "penitent" appeared. They seized the opportunity to show their gratitude for the good turn he had done them. But during the conversation, they learned there was a story behind the store they had not been told about. In fact, everyone in the family was not working, but stealing. Dragos turned beet red and headed towards the house, not wanting to hear any more details.

Carmen didn't want to know the family, but I visited a couple of weeks after I arrived. I met the grandmother, a woman over seventy who kept a tight hold on the reins of the household. "How do you have such beautiful skin?" I asked her.

"I live well here, Madame," she said. "I especially like the food."

Hospitable and open, the grandmother laid out almost all the food and drink she had in the house on the table, as if she wanted to show us how well off they were, but as gifts from the heart nevertheless.

We decided to visit Carmen and Dragos in Châteaudun. On the morning of our departure, we caught up with Jura. Kind as ever, he offered us a Pelforth beer, a beverage that unfortunately we have never come across again, and he put a turkey in our arms. He had grabbed it off the hook in a butcher's shop, he said. I took it to the butcher at the corner of our street, who offered "between neighbours" to cook it and have it ready before our return.

Jura said he had not seen or heard of Cristi since he suddenly stopped working for him. I'd been surprised when he and Melania disappeared from our hotel without a word. I treated them like my own children, I thought. I offered them what I could from the little I had. I miss them now.

There were a few hours before our train left, and as we waited I noticed that buses were pulling up to the station every few minutes, filling quickly, and leaving. Nobody was being asked for tickets when they got on.

"Let's get on too," I said, and in twenty minutes we were at the racecourse. It was a truly wonderful sight, with so many people running excitedly from the horse rings to the betting cages, and all the latest creations of Parisian fashion on display. It soon became overwhelming for me, though, seeing the despair of people weeping for their lost money – for a long time I was haunted by the devastation I saw on the faces of those who had bet such large sums I wondered how anyone could afford them.

At Châteaudun we were together again, even if only for a short time. I know I should have been glad, content in the moment, but I couldn't be. I was plagued with the constant worry about how long it would be until we met again, and about our futures. I didn't know then that happiness is measured in seconds that need to be cherished. At the time, my only thought was that the next day we would be returning to a situation I already knew to be uncertain. At our last meeting with Monsieur To, he had told us he couldn't pay for our hotel past the end of the month. What was to become of us? Where would we go?

The following morning we toured around the town and its

main attraction, the Château. Its walls rose from a rocky hill that on one side dropped into a deep precipice, and I would have loved to visit it. But the tickets were expensive and so, with great regret, I had to pass up an opportunity to explore a relic of the past, something which if possible should not be passed by.

When we left Jura he'd said he had a proposal for us we might be interested in. On our return we met him in front of the St. Antoine fountain where he let us know that in the coming January, he would be able to take Matei on in his team. It was now the end of September.

No matter how worried I was, I still enjoyed taking a walk around the surrounding streets; at least that didn't cost money. They seemed so very elegant, somehow, the old streets, with those famous little tables lined up in front of cafés, and people sitting at them with a cup of coffee, resting awhile or just chatting with their friends, writing or reading, or even just watching passers-by such as me.

With less than ten days till the end of month we paid our last visit to Monsieur To. That was the first time I noticed that next to his office was the Canadian immigration office. I asked him what he could tell us about it. "Nothing," he said, "except that it closed not long ago. Too bad you didn't think of it before, I could have helped you."

At the end of the month, on the morning of the last day that the hotel had been paid for, I woke with the thought of going to Germany. Winter was near; I couldn't expose a young child to the risk of being homeless. We were still waiting on that court hearing, sometime in the new year – we didn't even know what day yet. Matei tried to suggest a few options, but nothing he came up with was very reassuring. A Romanian he had met had promised him that although his place was very cramped, and he had a large family, we could stay there until Matei found work.

"No," I said. "First find work, then call us. If you want to come with us, come, if not, stay. Call us when you have something definite. It will be easier for you without us."

The train for Strasbourg left at nine. It was a terrible time. I felt bad knowing that Matei would be alone, penniless, with few acquaintances and no roof over his head. Doubt started to creep up on me, but feeling Anca's hand in mine, I knew we really had little choice. Our train arrived at noon, but before we reached our destination, I had to face the train guards. I had seventy francs in my purse. I didn't even think about buying tickets, which would have cost two hundred. An hour of embarrassment, guilt, fear and shame passed, and when the guards finally stopped in front of me, I confessed the truth. I needed forty francs for a phone card to call Aunt Valeria, so that left only thirty for emergencies. I had a child who I needed to feed, and I wasn't even sure Aunt Valeria was at home or that she could cross the border to come and get us.

One of the guards relented and signalled to the other to leave me alone. But the second one insisted. "She has to pay at least twenty francs. It's the law," he said. Later, after they had moved on and I had composed myself a little, I remembered one of the jokes about obeying the law that circulated during the Communist regime: the law is like a barrier; the coward passes under it, the smart person jumps over it and the stupid person stops in front of it.

There were no other problems, and a little after noon we reached our destination. I ran to the phone to contact Aunt Valeria, who promised to send her niece Nadia to get us. She wouldn't be there until after six in the evening, however. It was a nice late autumn day and the sun was still warm, so we went for a walk along the boulevard in front of the train station. We stopped on a bridge arching its back over the river that ran through the city and counted the many swans swaying on the waters. A sudden fear flashed through my mind, and I told Anca that if she wanted to speak to me, not to speak loudly. "Say it so that only I can hear," I warned her.

I knew that around any corner you could meet gypsies, Romanians, who had washed up here. I had by now heard and seen so many bad things some of my former countrymen were involved in, that I was scared we too would become targets if they heard our familiar language.

A Romanian saying goes, "You cannot escape what you fear." Unfortunately, the warning to me and to Anca came too late.

"Good afternoon, madam," I heard a voice behind me say. It was a man around fifty, tall and engaging. He started to tell me about his circumstances there and I let him talk without really listening. Finally he invited me to his place, or it could have been "their" place, I don't fully remember. But without too much thought I told him we were leaving at six and then we left as quickly as possible, back towards the train station. Near the station I discovered a little park and we sat down on a bench, watching the traffic and a few young women who seemed to be trying to get a lift. In my own country, these scenes were common in every city, intersections where people waited for a chance to hitch a lift to their destination. A middle-aged woman, plump but youthfully and very neatly dressed, sat down next to us on the bench. She would discreetly signal with her hand and cars would stop, then she would get up and speak to the driver. But after a short exchange she would return. "She probably can't find anybody going in her direction," I thought. She tried to start a conversation with me, but although I am talkative I am also wary of new people, and especially when alone in foreign places. At that moment a car stopped and I heard her ask, without getting up from the bench, "Combien?" After she got the answer she flew towards the car. It was only then that I finally understood what was really going on with those girls, and the men passing by in their cars.

It had started to get dark, so we returned to the station and looked for a free bench in the waiting room. There was none so we retreated to a sheltered corner from where I could watch the entrance. I felt I was being stared at and looked around to meet two lascivious eyes and a mouth twisted into a vulgar expression. I started to panic. It was already six and Nadia was nowhere to be seen. I looked around, hoping to see a police station or at least an open store. Nothing. "God," I prayed, "don't leave me," but I hadn't even finished that thought when the man we'd met at the bridge that afternoon appeared, with another man beside him. He reached out to Anca and offered her a candy bar, and then put his hand on my shoulder. "You can stay with us overnight if nobody comes. We live across the street." I shrugged his hand off but before I could respond, felt a touch on my back. Turning, I saw Nadia's friendly smile.

When we left Paris I hadn't thought about checking my passport. I had it with me at all times, but I hadn't checked the validity of the German visa, and it was only at the border crossing that I found it would expire in two days. I asked myself how the thought of leaving that day had popped into my mind just in time. Who had urged me to leave without delay? As time went on, I would note more of these "coincidences", as we usually call them.

It wasn't long before we were at Aunt Valeria's place, where of course she was waiting for us impatiently, eager to catch up again after all this time. I hadn't seen her since our return from Norway eighteen years previously. She looked unchanged to me, maybe thanks to that smile that remained as kind as ever, and the warmth in her eyes. She looked at me searchingly and I asked myself what she must have been thinking, although I don't think it would have been too hard to guess. Last time we met I was twenty-five, married, with a young family, returning home, but at least to a home. Now I was over forty, again with a child, and homeless. Aunt Valeria didn't let any of that sway her. She understood long before I did what mistake I had made. Now, as then, she only wanted to help me.

We stayed there for two weeks. Although I wrote to Matei, and thanks to Aunt Valeria's generosity I also sent him some money, I didn't hear anything back from him. I spent my time helping Aunt Valeria with the gardening and housework, or with Anca, or on walks into town. One day while looking at the goods displayed in the street I heard somebody close by speaking Romanian. I turned, and two young and pleasant figures looked back at me. They must have seen something in my face, because they tried to make me feel at ease. "Don't be scared," the young man said. "We're Romanian. I am Mihai and this is my wife, Mihaela."

As usual when immigrants meet, we shared our experiences. Everybody with "seniority" in refugee camps possesses a large lore of knowledge, which they convey to others in the hope they can help them. They told me about their predicament; he was an engineer, she was a paediatrician, and although in the past ten months they had tried everything they could think of, they didn't think they had a chance of remaining in Germany. So they had applied to emigrate to Canada.

"We also thought of trying for Australia," Mihaela said. We exchanged contacts, and two years later, I found out that's where they were.

Some time into my stay, Matei turned up, without warning. He was depressed. I knew how he felt, and it hurt me more when he started to tell me how he had been living all this time. He'd had to leave the hotel, but it turned out the Romanian man who had promised to host all of us couldn't even put Matei up. He met a few young men who were squatting in some unfinished apartment buildings and had little choice but to join them. There he saw the full raw picture of the many young people who, fed up with how bad things were in their home country, had simply left to "go West". They were following an unknown and treacherous path, and many had lost their way.

9

Finally, Matei had found work as a cleaner, and with the money he earned he had come to fetch us. "Where to?" I asked. He explained to me that he was fairly well paid and had found a room to rent for 2000 francs a month, somewhere near Paris.

After another tearful farewell with Aunt Valeria, the journey back seemed uneventful. Perhaps it was that this time I was less afraid, since we were going to a place where our stay was legal.

The landlady of our new accommodation was a young Algerian woman living with her daughter, who was about Anca's age. Our room was bare; no bed, no carpet or rug, no furniture, nothing, and we shared the bathroom and kitchen. Once again, I rummaged through our luggage, looking for something to make up a bed for Anca, while Matei and I slept on the floor in our clothes. It would do for the night, and the next day we would see what turned up.

The next day we met Laura, another countrywoman, who was also staying in the house. Laura was forty and was no beauty but she had an interesting face. She spoke fluent French, as well, which had helped her make some useful local connections. Some of these had helped her out with donations of furniture to set up her room, and, with more than she needed, she gave us some bits and pieces so we could make our room more homely.

Like most of us, Laura was just waiting for her lucky break, and in the meantime was pinning her hopes on Dan, a former prosecutor from Romania. She was hoping he would help her get that much-coveted legal status.

Matei was still working, but everything was temporary, and when the work ran out, well, I didn't want to think about it. Laura too was looking for work, and because she wouldn't take just anything she was often disappointed. We spent a lot of time together, and it seemed like she spent a lot of that time complaining about the landlady, whom she could understand a lot better than I could. She complained about Dan as well, but she couldn't decide yet whether to get rid of him since she didn't have anybody with better prospects. Dan was very arrogant and looked down on all of us as if we were delinquents. Perhaps it went with the job, that kind of attitude.

One Sunday morning I went down to the kitchen and immediately got the feeling that the landlady, Laura and Dan were waiting for me. Dan began with an aggressive and domineering tone.

"Why did you take our bread from the bag?"

At first I didn't believe he was talking to me. From the little that we had I would always offer something to everyone and the landlady was at our table every night, so she knew what we were eating. But it was me he was talking to. I turned to him and, in a voice that I tried my best to keep calm, said: "How dare you? Do you think you are still a judge in Romania?" Then I addressed the rest of them. "Shame on you! Shame on you for accusing me of such a thing."

I suspected the landlady had helped herself from their bag, but didn't say so. Dan, with his attitude and without any words to the contrary from the two women, had been drawn to the conclusion that I was the guilty party.

From then on our relationship with Laura was much more reserved. And even though we didn't expect any improvement in our circumstances, we weren't going to stay there longer than the month we had paid for. This upset the landlady, who made a big fuss about it, but that didn't change anything – we had decided to leave and that was that.

At the end of the month we headed to the Kopens. When we arrived, Andrei, without letting me explain anything, took a 500 franc note from his pocket and handed it to me. "Here, Elena. And don't think about paying it back."

Inside, Andrei had a proposal for us. "We've thought hard about this and decided that for as long as you need to stay here in France you can remain in our home. As you know, we come and go, and spend most of our time in our car. In fact right now we are getting ready for a trip to Holland, Germany and Greece. It would be a great help for us to have somebody at home so that the kids are not alone."

They didn't have to ask twice. That same night we were set up in one of the upstairs rooms in their home. The next morning I got the house keys, and in another two days it was just their kids and us. Matei wasn't working any more but he helped me with anything he could around the house until he was to start work in Jura's team.

I contacted Mrs. Mihailescu again, with whom I had kept in touch since we first arrived in Paris. I was saddened to hear, in both her words and her voice, that she had lost hope her daughter would recover. Less than a week later I heard the daughter had passed away. In the meantime her husband, who had stayed at home with their other child during the long hospitalisation, had arrived.

Laura also moved to Paris. Dan had had no more luck than the rest of us and so she had decided not to waste any more time with him. During a chance meeting in town Matei invited Laura to drop by, which she did. Her latest plan was that somebody had promised her a doctor for a husband, but since for the time being she had no money I never let her leave without a little gift bag.

The Kopen grandmother didn't live in the house any more, but she came by every night. She was in charge of supplies for the house and for us. I never asked where anything came from or let on that I knew, but she didn't make any secret of it. On the contrary she would tell us stories, filled with fun and light-heartedness, about the scrapes and narrow escapes that their life was so full of.

I was in constant touch with Dragos, and every time we spoke I felt he was unhappy knowing where I was. So I wasn't surprised that when he came to see us a little before Christmas, he suggested that we should move in with them into their new apartment in Chartres. I accepted, of course, but said moving would have to wait. Right then we were busy with Christmas preparations and trying to make everything look like "home". The Kopen children joined in, and everything went smoothly until the parents came back.

One morning shortly after their return, I was in the kitchen when I saw two policemen come through the front gate. They wanted to speak to the owner. When Andrei arrived they explained that a neighbour had complained about the noise from their dog.

Andrei invited the policemen in for coffee. During their

conversation I heard one of them say, "You have a very beautiful house. Do you mind if I ask what you do?"

"I'm a thief, sir." Andrei answered promptly. I froze, but all the policeman did was laugh. "That's a good one. You are funny, sir!"

Sometimes, it seems, when you tell the truth, you will hardly be believed. Perhaps the great majority of people believe what suits them, mostly out of convenience, rather than what they are actually seeing or hearing.

Later that day Laura visited us. She was very upbeat, and since I was very busy, I left her talking with Andrei. After a while I saw the two of them on the front steps of the house. I was just about to open the door to wish her goodbye when I heard my name. I stopped and listened, and my legs started to tremble when I heard the things she was saying. I couldn't believe it. Laura was someone I barely knew, who had helped us out, and here she was telling lies about me. I went up to our room to calm down a little, and later when I met him, Andrei said, "Elena, don't invite Laura here again. Anyway, I doubt she'll come." I never saw her again.

Christmas Eve, and the whole house was humming with the fervour of preparations for the big day. There was an abundance the likes of which I hadn't seen in a long time. The house was sparkling clean and grandly decorated, there were gifts for everyone, treats, lights, and on top of everything, those unforgettable aromas of baking, spices, fruits and the scent of pine drifting from the towering Christmas tree. The little girls ran around, delighted to have received white dresses full of lace and embroidery; they waited impatiently for Santa Claus' arrival and asked everyone what presents they thought they would get. Everybody in the house was happy – laughing, singing, dancing, drinking – it was complete merriment.

But in the midst of it all, I could not help feeling nostalgic for home. Quietly, I retreated to a darkened room and looked out through the windows. Everything I saw reminded me of my old life and everything that had been mine there. I looked with some jealousy at these people who seemed to have everything I had lost. But I didn't have time to sink too deeply into my thoughts. Noticing my absence, Andrei began searching, and soon found me. He was right. If my soul was troubled it was nobody else's fault; I had no right to affect others with my sorrow. So I put on a smile, and went out to join the fun.

The Kopens understood our desire to be together as a family, and on the first day of the new year we packed everything up once again and left for Chartres. At the apartment we found a fairly roomy kitchen, a bathroom and toilet, and a large room where we set up two double beds. All of this didn't mean anything compared to the fact that we were together. Of course our future was as uncertain as ever, but we were together and the belief never left me that together we would succeed.

Dragos would leave at four-thirty in the morning and return at night. Matei, who was now working on Jura's building team, stayed in a small room on site for the week, coming home on Friday nights. Carmen worked at a château and she and the girls she worked with had accommodation nearby. She too came home for weekends, and sometimes during the week as well. Anca and I stayed at home, learning French from the TV. The shows were very diverse, and during the almost three months we were alone at home, I became fluent in the language. On nice winter days I went into town, and almost always got as far as the cathedral. Its stone embroidery inspired awe in me, as it had and continues to do in many others.

Matei was earning reasonably good money and for once we managed to save something. We were still patiently waiting for our immigration case to be heard, now set down for the end of February. Matei met with one of the two female clerks of

Romanian origin who checked the details of each case. He left feeling bitter and resentful, however, when it became clear that if we could have paid something, we'd have had a better chance of a favourable decision. That was really when we lost hope in France. Not having offered the bribe, we anticipated what the outcome would be and so almost every night we were together, we made plans for leaving. A short time later, the bad news was confirmed; we could not stay in France.

Matei and I had different ideas about where to go, which we would examine from all sides until something that seemed interesting started to take shape. Matei's first suggestion was Spain, but he had no information other than what he'd heard from others. I was sick and tired of leaving for somewhere without the slightest idea of what I might find there, so Spain was out.

Dragos and Carmen, although not involved in these discussions at first, could obviously hear us from their bed in the same room. Then, two weeks after we did, they got the same negative result from their case review. They didn't seem as affected by it as we were, even though it had been unexpected.

One morning I heard Dragos say from the other bed: "Mum, we have to stick together. We knew we wouldn't be given the chance to stay but we wanted to surprise you. We're going to leave together."

I was overjoyed to think we would stay together, and called everyone to the table. "If we have to leave, there's no reason to waste any more time," I argued "Let's decide what to do." We sat down and started studying the world map.

That's how we came to remember Jean, the man who had already played a somewhat uneasy role in my life, and had still a bigger part to play. We needed help and we didn't know anybody else we could turn to. After Ion and I and the boys returned from Norway, we'd met him once, at a friend of his in Bucharest. I had no idea what had become of him, so despite my old misgivings, I phoned Remus, who succeeded in contacting Jean's friend, and so we got his contact details. He would help us, he said. All we had to do was find a way to reach Sweden.

We needed a good, roomy car, so Dragos and Matei went to Germany to look for one. They crossed the border by train. Although their entry visas to Germany had expired they still had their French ID cards, which while they weren't passports, were at least official documents. As at most border crossings in western Europe, customs and immigration checks were random. But since the fall of communist regimes in eastern Europe, more people could move freely about. Some western countries were experiencing an invasion of "gypsies" who didn't behave in a Christian fashion. Many of these types had dark complexions, and with his dark hair and skin, we knew there was a good chance Matei would be questioned at any border crossing.

This time however it was Dragos whom the customs officer approached. As he did, Dragos panicked, and when he tried to get his papers out of his jacket pocket, he pulled out all the money he had on him, about 30,000 francs. The notes scattered all over the ground, and although it could have all gone very wrong, fortunately the customs officer could see Dragos was genuinely distressed. He apologised and moved on without insisting on seeing their travel documents.

With the help of dear Aunt Valeria, Matei and Dragos found a sturdy and reliable Opel Senator, which was to carry us stoically wherever our travels took us. Dragos brought the car back by himself, Carmen and I packed everything we had into it, then one midnight we left France for Hausach.

We weren't stopped at the border this time, but I knew we would be eventually. We stayed in Hausach for a few days to prepare, in my case mostly spiritually, for our big gamble –

crossing first into Denmark, then Sweden, without any legal documents. I was very worried. We were not vagabonds, we'd never had any trouble with the authorities, but just looking at us now, I couldn't see how we could avoid the inevitable. I didn't want to tell anyone how I was feeling. We were all trusting in each other and I knew it would upset the others to talk about all the things that could go wrong. When you're young, you tend to believe that things will work out as you plan. I've come to understand that each of us plays only a small role in taking and carrying out decisions; through having our mind's eyes permanently open, we gradually learn to see more clearly beyond surface reality and so can better understand what needs to be done.

I remember Carmen saying, "What can they do to us? I'll tell them that we're going to visit our sick uncle. We still have our French documents; they can't know we're intending to stay." It all sounded so childish and I think they knew it too. But I didn't have any better ideas, so I kept my thoughts to myself.

At five in the morning we crammed into the car, surrounded by bags, pillows and other miscellaneous items that wouldn't fit in the boot or on the roof. We were heading north, to the Danish border. Before leaving I met Dragos in the hallway and couldn't stop myself from saying, "I don't know why, but I have a feeling things won't go easily. We should be prepared for that, no matter what."

10

WE STOPPED A FEW TIMES TO STRETCH AND TOWARDS
evening arrived at a small border village, Flensburg, where we
planned to stay until nightfall. We went into a pub to rest and have
a drink. A few people were sitting around tables playing cards,
someone was playing the piano, others were having some robust
discussion over their beer mugs. We sat down and a few people
tried to involve us in conversation, switching from German to
English, but unfortunately none of us could speak English either.
It is such an unpleasant predicament, being unable to
communicate with people, feeling completely fenced in and
helpless because you can't speak the language. Learning a
language cannot be achieved overnight. It is something that takes
time to do, that you need to be immersed in, and that wasn't
something our circumstances had allowed us to do.

We went for a walk and noticed that more people were moving
around on bikes and in horse-carts than in cars. The place was as
clean and orderly as anywhere in Germany, and there was a

peacefulness you could hardly believe still existed in this restless and noisy world.

Back in the car, we tried to find the road leading to the border point. We finally pulled over to find our location on the map, and a man came out from the store across the road. As he was getting into his car he began talking and gesturing at us. His meaning was clear: "You are not allowed to park on this street." Then, "There," he said, and pointed towards the embankment that rose in front of us. "At the end of the street is the border."

"Excuse us," Dragos replied in German. This was one of the few phrases he had learned during the time he had stayed with Aunt Valeria. We were almost ready to thank him for the information, despite the telling off we'd received. We had learned what we wanted, and after waiting till he went away we drove up the hill and then down on the other side. In front of us stretched a few roads and, since "forward" was our motto, we picked the one leading straight ahead.

After a few hundred metres that we covered in great fear we saw the sign that worried us the most: "Forbidden"; along with the words that made us the happiest: "Border". We all read them at the same time, out loud. We began to advance cautiously, in considerable trepidation, trying to think of a plausible answer in case somebody stopped us. For no very good reason we decided that, if we were stopped, we would speak only Romanian and use body language to say we were lost. We covered a significant distance, or maybe because we were so emotional it just felt like it, when finally in the dark we were able to make out the familiar border sentry box and next to it, the barrier. Everything seemed to be deserted, and to our delight, the sentry box was empty. Carefully, Dragos, Carmen, and Matei all climbed out, lifted the barrier, and waited for the car to pass. Then they realised there was nobody to drive it, as I was holding Anca asleep in my arms. Our laughter relaxed us and joyfully we drove on.

Suddenly, I thought of something. "Are you sure we are in Denmark?" Perhaps they had moved the border crossing, I thought. Only after seeing a few signs in Danish did we finally calm down.

At the first settlement we stopped at a motel and took a single room. Even though I was exhausted and desperately wanted to fall asleep, my eyes wouldn't close. Will tomorrow be as lucky for us? I kept asking myself.

There was no land border between Denmark and Sweden. In the morning we crossed the Jutland peninsula, boarded the ferry for Odense, then took another ferry to Copenhagen Island and headed towards Helsingor, all without encountering any difficulties. A little after noon we were on the ferry between Helsingor, Denmark and Helsinborg, Sweden. The customs checkpoint was less than a hundred metres from the shore, and we lined up behind the other cars from the ferry.

This was our first serious encounter with the authorities, and though they tried to be helpful by speaking English, there was no need for me to know English to understand they didn't accept our story. I think they were very puzzled by the fact that we had knowingly put ourselves in this situation; why had we shown up at a border crossing without any valid document?

We were led to an office and told to wait. After more than an hour, we were escorted by four policemen onto the same ferry we had arrived on. When we disembarked back in Helsingor, we were delivered to the Danish authorities. A police officer climbed in and took the wheel of our car, while we were taken to a van. Before long we were at the police headquarters. Opposite the offices were several cells, all empty, and we were happy that we weren't put in one of them. Instead we were shown a bench on which we all squeezed together to discuss our situation in bitter whispers.

All of us were on edge because nobody was telling us anything. We started to blame one another for what had happened. Tired, hungry and thirsty, Anca was crying. It was like the nightmare of facing an exam for which you are not prepared. We kept pushing Carmen, who had the best English, to ask what they intended to do with us. After two hours of this agony we would have preferred anything to happen just to see a change. Finally, we were put in a car, but without being told where we were going. We couldn't see out, we couldn't make out anything in the surrounding darkness, and I could feel a dark cloud descending into our souls. Matei finally broke the heavy silence. "Stay calm. After all, what can they do to us? We tried to cross the border in broad daylight, in plain sight. It's not as if we're criminals. They can see that. Besides, I've heard that here the jails are pretty comfortable."

The van stopped, but only Carmen, Anca and I were allowed out. Dragos and Matei were driven off, without our knowing where. I didn't like this new development, but didn't have time to think much about it before we were led to a long, low building, standing under bright lights. The door was unlocked and we entered a room with a few beds in it. Next door was another room where there were a few milk cartons and some fruit on a table. From this second room, a door led to the toilet and another room, the door of which was locked. All the windows were barred.

The door we entered was locked also, and we realised we were under arrest. Anca soon fell asleep after drinking some milk, while Carmen and I tried to create a more comfortable resting place. We put two beds together, hunted through the blankets to find a couple that seemed least used, and settled down to rest.

It was impossible to sleep. The room was dismal and alien.

From time to time a new person would come in and then a discussion would start, with the others wanting to learn what had happened to them, and asking for news of their loved one. I climbed up on the bed to look out the window. I could see other buildings in the compound, and a wire fence separating them from a road. Although it was well after midnight, lots of people were coming and going, most of them passing through a gate next to the one we had come through, after presenting a document to the officer at the entrance. I could make out a few metres of open ground on the other side of the fence. Beyond that, I suspected, was just a field. I scrutinised every corner, looking for a possibility of escape, without knowing how I could possibly do that. I couldn't reconcile myself to the idea that I was imprisoned, and the desire for freedom fired my imagination. Then I turned my head to Anca, now sleeping peacefully, and understood I would have to wait. I was coming to grips with the reality that I was no longer in control of things, that nothing that I thought should be done was in my power to do.

Every one of the new arrivals had made an illegal attempt to cross the border, which they confessed to those around them in the greatest detail. By morning the room was crowded, but the majority of people didn't seem to be bothered about where they had ended up. Instead, they seemed to know what was going to happen. I got the sense they were optimistic, waiting for the morning when everything would get settled. How, I didn't know.

At least we had a bed. In the morning breakfast was brought in and then the restless waiting commenced. At about ten thirty, we were taken to a courtyard, then to another building in the compound. Our spirits lifted when we got a glimpse of our car; it was like seeing a family member who, knowing something was amiss, was patiently waiting for us. In the new building was everybody we'd seen the night before, sitting in a line of chairs.

Every half an hour or so a police officer would appear, followed by an interpreter. He would call a name and then they would leave together with the "lucky one", as we thought.

We sat in front of the door, each time hoping to hear our name, but lunch was served and the hall was almost empty, and still our names were not called. I was restless and couldn't understand how Carmen could sit so calmly, doing a drawing with Anca. Finally we were the only ones left. The officials we could see approaching us couldn't be coming for anybody else. One of them addressed us in Romanian, "Your husbands have asked for political asylum, but we need your acceptance. Do you agree?"

Of course we did. My heart lit up with hope now. I forgot all my anger at waiting and felt every fibre of my body relaxing as I sat down to ask myself, "Are we truly free?" I saw myself beyond the wire fence, where the ones who had been accepted lived. I saw ourselves established in our future home. What joy! I was dreaming up a whole new life while one of the two officials was talking on the phone, when suddenly the words, "We are sorry," woke me up.

"What is it, Carmen?" I asked.

"From what he says, it seems Denmark is not accepting us; the decision has been changed."

And so we were led back to the room we had left in the morning hoping never to return to. I didn't know how long we would be staying there. No decision had been made about us and nobody was telling us a thing. I paced like a caged lion, boiling with anger, not thinking of Carmen and me but of the fact that a child was forced to stay in such inhospitable conditions. We climbed on the beds to better see out into the courtyard, and I saw one of the two men with whom we had had our meeting earlier passing in front of our window. He had left me with a very good opinion of him and now I thought he might help us. What did I want? Ever since we arrived, I had seen a door that never opened and I suspected that behind it could be another room or a bathroom. Before he came in, I told Carmen, "Ask him to help us, to see what he can do to improve our conditions a little. We don't know how long they're going to keep us here and we need a bed, blankets and a bathroom."

It worked. The door was unlocked and I saw I hadn't been wrong; behind it was another room, with beds, lots of sheets and another bathroom. Nobody else went in, which made me think that while it was a privilege, it meant we would be staying here a while. We went back to the adjoining room when meals were served. There were a lot of books in our new room as well, and though we didn't understand much, they helped us invent stories for Anca.

We stayed in this room for four days without any news from the outside, with only our thoughts which gradually became more and more sombre. I envied the people I saw through the window walking freely about. We looked longingly at our car, which also seemed to be missing our company. The car was where, sad, happy and noisy, we had been spending the greatest part of our time together recently; we ate, laughed, even slept there and formed plans for fulfilling our dreams.

In the afternoon of the fourth day we were put in a car. Again we had no idea where we were going, but as always we were hoping for the best. When we got out, we were in front of the Copenhagen police headquarters. This is new, I thought, something is going to happen. But what? We found Matei and Dragos in a hall waiting for us, and I could see the unhappiness on their faces. "What is it?" we both asked. "Were you badly treated? What's wrong"

"No, we were in a prison with regular detainees, but treated differently and in separate cells. But that's not the problem.

Denmark has refused our request to be accepted in a refugee camp so we are to be deported to Poland. But first, we have to sign a form saying that this is our wish and we accept the decision."

"What do you mean?" exclaimed Carmen. "We should sign that we want to be deported?"

"Yes, sign that we give up our request to stay," said Matei. "I don't want to do it, but Dragos has already signed."

"What chance do we have if we don't sign?" I asked

"None," answered Dragos. "There's no point in resisting, because one way or another they will find a reason to deport us."

11

WE WERE SCARED, SO WE TRIED TO CONVINCE MATEI TO SIGN. He got angry, but since nobody was on his side he finally accepted he had no choice. He asked for a travel document to use on our way home, because he no longer had a passport. He was eventually given something, and in an hour we were on a ferry bound for Szczecin, Poland.

We still had our car, and our money. The police had paid our fares – all that was left for us to do was to book two cabins where we could rest. I felt an overwhelming desire to relax, and we headed towards the buffet, where, much against my usual practice, I drank two bottles of beer. To be honest I could have drunk more, just to forget that from the next morning, we didn't know what road we would take.

In the morning we quarrelled with the Polish immigration officers, who wouldn't accept Matei despite his document from the Danish police. We had to wait more than two hours before they would let him out of the building. Finally we were free – but in the wrong country. We headed to town, and since it had never entered our heads to follow the Danish authorities' advice and return to Romania, Carmen spread the map of Europe on her knees, and traced the border between Poland and Germany. There didn't seem to be an obvious crossing point, so we took a hotel room to think calmly about what we should do.

The first step was to contact Jean. He said it shouldn't be too hard to come and help us, depending on what we expected of him. He could speak fluent Danish, Swedish and Norwegian, and, knowing that at the border crossing generally only the driver is asked for documents, we didn't see any obstacle in heading to Sweden if he was driving the car.

"We have to try," we said. But gradually we came to realise that Jean didn't really empathise with the situation we were in, or if he did, he couldn't really be bothered making any effort himself. It was very easy to make promises and keep postponing delivery on them, but we couldn't just keep waiting.

So we resumed our search for a way into Germany. This wasn't an easy problem to solve, and we ended up staying in the hotel a lot longer than we had expected to. Fortunately inflation was running very high at that time in Poland. Since the Iron Curtain fell all across eastern Europe there were signs of the struggle for economic recovery. One of them was that foreign currency was king. With our francs and Deutschmarks we were treated like millionaires; the only time in our whole odyssey across Europe when we were treated differently than as wretched, stateless migrants.

We had a pretty good idea of how checkpoint inspections were carried out, but wanted to reassure ourselves, so we drove out to the border one day and watched. My hunch was confirmed; it was only the driver who produced any documents. An idea sprang to my mind. We stopped a few cars and tried to tell the occupants what we wanted: somebody to drive our car across to the other side. They listened to us, but I think it was hard for them to believe, to understand what we wanted them to do and why. I suppose we were asking them to smuggle us across the border, which seems now a rather bold suggestion to make to strangers. That may have been why they had such trouble understanding. When your own situation is stable and secure, taking or being asked to take such a risk is a lot to try and comprehend.

Some workers approached us. We had seen them when we first arrived, working at a construction site across the road. Two of them came over, and, in bad English, told us, "We know what you want. If you give us 300 Deutschmarks, we'll help you cross. But one of you will have to stay here with the car." Curious, we set up a meeting for four in the afternoon in front of our hotel. The two showed up, and right away they asked for the money. "No," said Dragos, "We'll follow you and you'll get the money there, not here."

"You should trust us. You Romanians and we Polish are both gypsies."

"What did you say?" Matei exploded. "Maybe you are, but what do you know of Romanians?" And then, turning on us, he carried on. "Why in the heck aren't you saying anything? What do these people know about us? What do they know of the Romanian soul, Romanian culture? Let's go, before I beat them into a pulp."

Matei's outburst aside, we were saddened and ashamed at the remarks the Polish workers had made. Romanians were an intelligent, talented and above all gentle people. We were very proud of our Latin origin, and we had nothing in common with gypsies. I say strongly that I am not racist; and because I am touching on this subject again, I want to be clear on what I know of the presence of gypsies in Romania. Gypsies came to Romania from India in the fourteenth century and lived first as slaves on landowners' estates, alongside our serfs. Many had uncommon musical talents, and they learned our songs of joy and grief. In this way they eased their existence, which was as wretched and oppressed as that of our own serfs. As the years went on, their lives slowly changed for the better, until they had the same rights as the Romanian people.

Now, Dragos turned back to the Polish men. "Go ahead and we'll follow you."

I couldn't understand how he could make a deal with this kind of people, but at the first intersection I saw him change course, quickly losing them on the city streets. After a while we were headed for the Czechoslovakian border.

"Those guys took us for fools if they believed for a moment we would follow them. Did you really believe me?" Dragos asked me.

During the past few days I hadn't been well. A boil had appeared in a rather delicate place, and besides the temperature I was running, any movement was causing me pain. Now, the broken surface of the road was causing me real discomfort. It was dark by the time we took the road to Gorzov, and after a day of running around none of us was in a good mood. Darkness and bad roads, and the exhaustion of a full day made us downcast and moody. We were silent, each lost in our own thoughts about what to do, when into the silence, Carmen began to sing a party song. I soon joined in and we continued with many more songs from home that made me ask myself once more, What am I doing here? My soul was, is and will always be at home in Romania. What brought me here and why? Could I really endure all this? It was past midnight when we finally stopped at a hotel.

In the morning we did some shopping. We couldn't help noticing the desolate atmosphere of the town; the buildings, ugly and disfigured by coal smoke, were simply depressing. The streets and pavements were bare of any greenery, there were no parks, nothing. It was as if a malevolent spirit had passed through and punished the town and people for some unknown reason.

We reached the Jelenia Gora border crossing into Czechoslovakia, where to our surprise we learned that our visas had expired a few days before. I had never checked our documents, but I was surprised that Dragos, who was normally meticulous about these things, hadn't said something. I kept calm, relying on him to sort things out. Suddenly I realised he was whistling at me through his teeth, "Boil!" At the same time, the customs officer was saying, "I am sorry, it's not possible."

Terrified by the prospect of being locked up again, I was emboldened. "I'm sick," I told him in Romanian. Carmen translated, and I understood the answer: he wanted papers, proof. I walked to his booth and started to unbutton my skirt, demonstrating with gestures that I would show him. As I hoped, he stopped me before I got too far.

"What is she doing, what is she doing?" He turned towards Carmen.

"Showing you proof," she said.

"No, no, no! Not necessary. Pass, pass!" he exclaimed. And he stamped "free pass" on our documents.

We breathed a sigh of relief when we crossed onto Czechoslovakian soil. Everything was different, the houses were nice and clean, everything seemed brighter and we felt more welcome. We drove on a well-paved highway against a beautiful mountain landscape. It was like passing from the yard of a careless or lazy tenant into one kept by someone keenly interested in what passers-by might think. We still didn't know what we were going to do, but being in a nicer environment helped us relax, so we could think.

I thought we should look for a small border village, from where it might be easier to cross to the other side. We agreed to look for such a place, but first needed to eat. The stores were well stocked and clean, service was prompt and it was hard to ignore the difference in living standards compared with where we had just come from. I thought how anyone who visited our country would get the same bad impression, now that the disastrous fallout from the communists could be seen more clearly than ever. People had been unable to do anything to improve matters for so long, there was nothing they could do other than enjoy each new joke ridiculing the politicians of the time.

Carmen, Anca and I headed for the food stores. Dragos and Matei headed for those with technical equipment; we agreed to meet back at the car. I was in a good mood, Anca was happy we were going to Aunt Valeria's, to live in a "real" house and sleep in a nice bed. It was late when, after buying a lot of delicacies, we returned to our meeting place. Everybody was there except Matei, but we didn't fret, thinking he would soon show up. After an hour I set off along the streets looking for him, but with no result. Finally, after another hour, he showed up, his happy face contrasting strongly with ours. I poured out on him all the waves of frustration that had kept me tense for so long, but to my surprise he didn't react as I expected and only listened to me quietly.

We pressed on, and my anger had melted away somewhat, when the tune of a Romanian dance song rang out. Matei had bought a harmonica on his little adventure, and was now playing it skilfully. He had wanted one for a long time, and, making enquiries from store to store, he finally found one – a long way from our agreed meeting point.

We were together again, we had discussions, we got angry, exchanged opinions, made plans. Ideas floated around like autumn leaves and then everything would stop when we seemed to be onto something. Then we would all inspect it to see what it was, if it would work, whether we could make it any better. We passed through Prague, then Pilsen, and late in the day arrived at the small border village on which we had set our hopes. We headed directly to the frontier line to weigh our chances, taking a road that led deep into the woods. Finally, seeing nothing other than a few houses, we reached the point where a marker showed us that across the path, through the woods, was Germany.

"Look, Mum, Germany," said Dragos. "I know you are brave. One step and you are there."

Indeed, nobody seemed to be around, but we couldn't do anything seeing as we had to take the car across as well. We returned the way we'd come, and I think everyone suffered the helpless feeling of not being able to cross to the other side when everything looked so close, so tempting. To look through the forest and know that the place we wanted so badly to get to was just a few hundred metres away was hard.

At the first house on our way back we saw on old man leaning over the fence. He was the first human being we had seen there, so we stopped. Dragos and Carmen tried to make themselves understood, but although he seemed well disposed, he couldn't understand French or English, and they returned disappointed to the car.

I don't know what made me say, "I won't leave without speaking to him myself," but I got out and approached the man, and greeted him in Romanian.

"Good day," he replied. "What brings you to these places?"

I couldn't believe what I was hearing. "How do you know Romanian?"

"Oh, from the war. I ended up there for a while. But tell me, how can I help you?"

I explained to him that we wanted to cross to the other side and needed help.

"I can help you cross, but not in the car."

"We'll pay you," I told him.

"It's not a question of money; it's just that I can't. It would be best to go to my neighbour." He pointed to a house not far from his. "There, there's a woman who can help you better than I. And she speaks Romanian too."

His neighbour greeted us with a wide, warm smile as if she had been expecting us for ages. Everything about her reminded me of the familiar Romanian hospitality; with open arms, she pushed us towards a large table in front of a bed.

"Come in, come in, sit down and I will bring you food. You're probably all hungry." She started opening cupboards and setting on the table everything she had in the house: stuffed eggs, fried chicken, sausages, ham, cheese, plum brandy, wine. Everything tasted so good, and we were so grateful for her hospitality. But we couldn't forget what we had come for. When I explained, she calmed us down.

"Just drink, eat, and we'll come up with something. I'll call my husband in from the fields."

Her husband appeared with mud on his trousers and boots and a tired and sweaty face, but with immense kindness in the big, open smile that lit up his face. While he changed, his wife explained our predicament to him.

"Our son is a customs officer," he told us. "Let my wife and I go and talk to him right now and ask his opinion." They came back in half an hour. "Legally it can't be done. But ten or eleven kilometres from here we have a relative who is a priest. He has helped others cross the border, so we'll go and see him."

His wife chipped in. "First my husband and somebody from your group will go and the rest can wait. I'm calling him now."

"I think you're the best suited to plead our cause," Dragos said to me. "I'll come with you." Carmen, Anca and Matei stayed back.

It didn't take us long to reach the priest's house – just long enough to fully admire the beauty of the road that seemed to have been cut through the heart of the fir tree forest. The priest opened the door; he was short and skinny, with a beard, like all Orthodox priests. And like most, he didn't smile a lot. But he was sympathetic. He invited us to sit at the kitchen table by a well-heated hearth and listened to our story.

"You've convinced me," he said finally, "but you'll also have to talk with my wife. She doesn't agree with my involvement in these things – and of course, my life would not be worth living if I did something she did not approve of."

I stood up and followed the priest's gesture down a dark corridor that led to a yard, where his wife was feeding her poultry and pigs. I assumed she knew why we were here, and I wasn't up to telling the same story all over again, so on a hunch I took 200 marks from my pocket and handed it to her.

"Thank you!" I said. "We were in such need of help and you understood us."

"That's fine," she said, without lifting her head. "You're welcome to stay the night here, too, if you like."

While Dragos went back to get the others, I sat down and started to peel potatoes for supper.

It began to rain. "You know, we could cross tonight," the priest said. "This weather could help you. Nobody patrols in such weather."

The rest of our group arrived, and on hearing the proposal, quickly agreed to it. But I wasn't in favour.

"I'm not going to cross," I said. It's pitch black, it's pouring and we have a child with us."

They listened, and we agreed we would cross the following evening. After a sleepless night, at dawn I went for a walk around the village, waiting for the others to wake up.

"You have the whole day free," the priest told us, "and tonight at six we'll meet so that I can show you the road you have to take. There's a soccer game tonight between our village and the village across the border. It's almost certain that most of the men, including the border guards, will be at that."

We left our car with him, having agreed he would take it over when we got word to him that we'd made it safely.

"What are we going to do with Anca?" I asked. She was too young to walk any distance. Then Matei had an idea.

"We'll put her in the backpack!" He cut two holes in the sides of one our packs for her legs, and arranged it so it would be just like sitting on a little stool carried on her dad's back. I explained to her that she wasn't to cry or to talk loudly or we would end up back in the little room where we had stayed for those four long days.

The priest gave me some old track pants and well-used boots, which were much more appropriate for the conditions than anything I had. I took only a few essentials. Everything else we left in the car.

12

At six o'clock we were at the edge of the forest, where the priest tried to draw directions in the air. "Go straight for about two kilometres, then left for about three, then you are on your own. God be with you!"

The hill ahead of us was bare, so we climbed quickly to reach the forest where we would have better cover. Dragos and Carmen got away quickly, running up the hill, followed by Matei with Anca on his back. I followed, but I was very tired, and my legs were like lead. I fought hard, but in my borrowed clothes it was like struggling through heavy mud. I fell far behind the others, and lost sight of them as soon as they entered the forest.

I caught them up as they tried to work out what direction we should go next. I didn't make any suggestions, as directions weren't my strong point, and Dragos also stayed quiet. It fell to Carmen and Matei to decide. It was getting dark as we set off again, this time at a much slower pace. The earth was soft, and fallen trees and branches blocked our path. For a good part of the way we also had to watch for what remained of 40-year old barbed wire fences.

They made me think with horror of the dangers faced by those in the past who had wanted to escape the much-touted paradise. At least no one would be shooting at us.

The forest began to clear, and while it was easier to walk we weren't totally happy with the change as we felt much more exposed. We came across a road stretching away on our left. Matei was adamant we had to cross it – he was right, as it turned out – but Carmen wanted to go straight ahead. We didn't have time to think long before headlights lit up the road. We barely had time to take cover behind trees before the car rushed past. Now Anca wanted to get down; she needed to go to the toilet. Dragos and Carmen didn't have the patience to wait and took off along the road. When Anca had finished, Matei and I followed and tried to catch them. But they had vanished. We kept heading in the direction they had run, and before long we reached another road, this time curving away to our right and continuing through the middle of the woods. We were lost. We had no idea where the cars were coming from and where they were going. Were we in Germany or still in Czechoslovakia?

We got onto the highway, and, avoiding any headlights, crossed it and entered the forest on the other side. We could just hear some dogs barking; at least that meant we were close to a settlement. Anca asked to get down again, and this time she started to cry. I cuddled her and asked her to make no noise, so nobody would know we were there, and told her that in a short while we would meet Dragos and Carmen. While I was talking to her, a car, seemingly the same one we had seen before, came onto the road from the other side of the forest, where we had parted company with Dragos and Carmen.

Worried we had been seen we put Anca back in the backpack and started to walk parallel to the highway, but in the woods, in the same direction most of the cars were going. When we couldn't see any headlights we walked along the road, where it was easier going. As soon as any light appeared we dove into the woods. Often we only just had time to drop into the ditch to avoid being caught in the headlights.

More lights appeared in front of us, and we waited for the vehicle to drive past. But nothing came. We turned back into the forest and sat down to wait. By now we were very scared; all the noises we heard were made by patrols, and we could picture ourselves being arrested. Still the car did not come, so finally Matei decided to set out on a reconnaissance trip.

Anca began to fret quietly. "Where is daddy, where are the dogs we can hear, what if they come closer?" Matei soon returned, and with good news. The lights were from a car parked in front of a house. If we were quick, we could reach the other side of the highway and continue on our way.

Following the same rules as before, we kept walking, until at last I saw a sign. I crossed myself and breathed a sigh of relief when I was close enough to read *Zimmer*. We were in Germany, in front of an establishment offering rooms for rent.

What a relief! My spirits lifted so strongly it was a physical sensation, like the removal of Anca from her backpack must have felt for Matei. I was overwhelmed with happiness and a pleasant calm, the fear and tension of a night-time border crossing, through a dark, unknown forest draining away to be replaced with hope.

I stayed with Anca while Matei went into the hostel to call the priest in Czechoslovakia. He came out happy, telling me Dragos had also called him just a little while before. The priest would bring the car over the same night.

"Where to?" I asked.

"He told me to call him later. But the owner of this place has offered to take us to the next town for only ten marks."

"Why?"

"He asked me what I wanted, and I told him I needed to call someone in Czechoslovakia, that I had come from France and had left the car on the road when it broke down. So he offered to help us out."

In ten minutes we were on a narrow street flanked by smart shops. It was past midnight and quiet all around, so it wasn't hard to hear Dragos's voice.

"Mum." I looked around and saw him at one of the windows of the hotel in front of us. In no time we were face to face, in the hallway.

"Hey, you had better hide yourself," he told me. "If the owner sees you he'll think we're highway robbers."

"Why? What's wrong?"

"Have a look in the mirror."

I couldn't help but laugh at what I saw in the mirror at the end of the hallway: a woman with leaves and twigs in her hair, in torn boots, her trousers covered in mud and more leaves.

Dragos and Matei went to the reception desk to show their French cards, which were now the only identification documents we had. But the owner didn't want to see them; it seemed he understood our situation. We called Czechoslovakia one more time to let the priest know the address, and he said he'd be there before morning.

We washed, threw the ruined clothes into the garbage and sat down to compare notes. Dragos and Carmen had followed the same path we did, stopped at the same motel, and asked to make a phone call as we had. Neither of them noticed the border guard sitting at one of the tables until his dog approached Carmen. They didn't know what miracle happened next, but somehow the guard left them alone. Carmen's nerves suffered so badly she had to go outside to recover. Dragos made the phone call, and when the owner asked, "Where are you from?" he'd answered, "From France, our car broke down, we left it up the road and...."

Now I understood why the proprietor had offered to bring us here, without asking any questions. It was a mystery – another one of those lucky coincidences – how Dragos and Matei had come up with the same story, without any advance planning.

Dragos and Matei stayed by the window all night, but by seven in the morning the priest had still not shown up in our car. They called again and set up a meeting for noon at Weiden train station. Our thinking was to get as far away from the border as we could, as quickly as possible. The first bus for Weiden left the station behind our hotel at eight. We hurried through breakfast and ran to the bus, reaching Weiden an hour later. From there, at twelve-thirty, a train was leaving for Hausach, 400 kilometers away. Either the car would arrive, or we'd take the train. Ten minutes before the train left we bought tickets. Matei stayed behind to wait.

It was a long journey, but was nothing compared with the terrors we had gone through to get into Germany. At eight in the evening we got off, to find Matei waiting for us. The priest had brought the car only a few minutes after our departure. On the road to Aunt Valeria's, we shared our stories about the routes we'd taken. Soon we were safe, welcomed once again with open arms. We immediately contacted Jean, who promised to come in less than a week. It was now the beginning of April, a little before Easter.

I don't know what evidence Matei had for his conviction, but he had always considered himself a lucky man. While we waited for Jean to appear, every day Matei would go into town, and one day he arrived back in front of the house in a taxi. We still had some money, but not enough to afford a taxi.

"Don't say anything, please," he said, seeing I was ready to ask the question. "I wanted to feel human, like a man living a normal life. Do you remember, when still in Paris, I wrote to a clairvoyant? She told me that I would win something, without specifying what. I didn't want to tell you since you would have laughed in disbelief. But, well, I won... the lottery. Look, a thousand marks. I told you I was lucky."

Good fortune had to be celebrated, and so we left for Baden-Baden with Aunt Valeria, and the following evening stopped at a Greek restaurant, visited Offenburg and spent another day at an amusement park in Kehl. We didn't know what the future had in store for us, but this mini-vacation was like an oasis of normality, lifting our spirits even if briefly above the continuing uncertainty about our future.

Once more we contacted Jean. He again promised to help us, and this time he finally came to meet us. Eleven years had passed since I had last seen him at the Oslo train station. Although he hadn't been of any practical help then, we were now certain he was our only hope. So the signal that should have rung alarm bells for us was caught by Aunt Valeria. Like me, she didn't like the way he was always trying to hide behind his glasses. I was annoyed by his endless prevarication, and the fact he didn't contribute at all to our plans, even though he was a key part of them. We agreed we would meet him in Frederikshavn, in the north of Denmark, and together we would take the ferry to Göteborg, Sweden.

Jean left the next day, and in a few days more we farewelled Aunt Valeria again, heading for the same border crossing as last time. The morning before leaving I met Dragos in the hallway, who noticed my uneasiness.

"Don't say anything," he said. "Let's just see how things turn out." So although I did have something to say, I kept it to myself.

We reached the same embankment as before, but it wasn't as easy to find the road we took on our first attempt. By mistake or through our impatience we got onto a different path. We eventually found the same empty booth, however, and this time the barrier was up, as if it was waiting for us and inviting us in. We drove on, and very late at night reached a motel. I stayed in the car with Anca while the others headed to the reception desk. Although it was open, there was no one there. I picked Anca up and we all looked around everywhere in the hope of finding someone. There was nobody. Eventually we found a few bedrooms with beds stacked on top of one another. We each chose one, took a shower and fell into bed exhausted.

I don't know how long we slept, but it was still dark when I heard Dragos say, "I think we should leave, we have a long journey ahead of us." When we took our places in the car, it was five a.m. We were still groggy with sleep, but there still seemed to be nobody around.

We headed north up Jutland Island, to Frederikshavn, where we found a motel near the harbour. I had already started to fret at the thought of what was going to happen. However, as agreed, Jean arrived around lunchtime. It was decided that we would take the eight-thirty ferry that night, as foot passengers. The car would be brought over by a friend of his who lived nearby. When we dropped the car off with them, they seemed kind and understanding.

Still, the fear was building within each of us. We boarded the ferry, to endure three more hours of anxiety. Each of us coped with it differently. I walked to and fro, while the others emptied a bottle of vodka. Knowing how passport control was operated I feared most for Matei. The rest of us looked passable as locals, with Dragos and I blonde and blue-eyed, and Carmen blonde from a bottle. Anca was just a child, of course, but we couldn't hide Matei. Jean advised him to mix in with a group of children and to carry Anca in his arms.

The waiting was over. With my head shrunk between my shoulders and well aware of how little chance there was for all of us to get past without any difficulty, I squeezed in among the first in the stream of people weaving along the corridor and between the customs officers on each side of the gangway. I passed, and went on to the first floor of the building from where I could clearly see what was happening downstairs. Carmen and Dragos had their arms around each other, and were kissing and cuddling as they walked through. Jean followed them. We waited. Still Matei did not show, and nor did Anca. As the flow of people dwindled I knew something had gone wrong.

Eventually Jean left to find out what had happened, and he came back with the news we'd been dreading. Matei had been stopped. Worse than that, Jean had witnessed an incident in which, when one of the customs officers had tried to get Anca out of his arms, Matei had knocked him down with a left jab. Someone asked him whether he was alone and what he wanted. He said he was with us and that we all wanted to stay here.

Then I saw Matei, accompanied by a policeman. "My wife should be here somewhere," he was saying.

I ran into the street, crying desperately. Jean followed me and tried to calm me down, promising he would intervene and at least get Anca out. Mindlessly, I set off down the late night streets. Dragos and Carmen followed, trying to console me.

"We're all in the same boat. We're suffering with you. We'll do something," they said.

I knew they were, but it was so hard, after all we'd been through, to think how close we'd come, for everything now to go wrong.

We returned to the ferry terminal house and I saw Jean holding Anca by the hand. I breathed a sigh of relief. Matei's situation would be resolved, and anyway we didn't intend to leave without him. Tomorrow we'd sort things out.

Then Jean told us we couldn't stay at his house. The police had his address, he said, but he would arrange for a friend, a Romanian, to put us up for a night. We were to meet the next morning at his place.

Why, if the police knew his address anyway, could we not stay there now? What difference did it make? These were questions I only asked myself much later. At the time, we couldn't stop and analyse what seemed mere details.

It was two in the morning when we met Dan, an agreeable young man who sincerely wanted to help us out. But, with some embarrassment, he explained he would have a fight on his hands to convince his wife, Doina.

On our way to his house, we were stopped by the police. I froze, thinking they were looking for us. But it was only a routine late-night check and Dan was able to reassure the officers. At his house, Dan's mother-in-law welcomed us. She had just arrived from Romania for a visit. Then Doina appeared.

"This is none of our business," she said. "I don't want to hear it." Dan pointed out that we had a child with us, that it was nearly three o'clock, and that we had to leave for Jean's at seven. She didn't say any more, but she did everything she could to make sure she wouldn't see us again. Her mother, though, sorted out a place for us to sleep, and in the morning, prepared something for us to eat. Before we left for Jean's, Dan allowed me a few minutes to call Remus in Romania.

"Don't tell me anything. I know everything," he said.

"What? What do you know?" I asked.

"I had a dream. You wanted to cross into Sweden and you got caught, right?" I couldn't believe it. He'd dreamed exactly what happened.

On our way to Jean's apartment, Dan told us we should have gone to Norway. Dragos disagreed, but their discussion was interrupted by the sight of our car in front of Jean's apartment building. Only one member of our family was still missing. I was still hoping things would work out, but I knew it couldn't happen. I'd hardly finished washing myself and Anca when there was a knock on the door.

Jean didn't appear surprised. "I think it's the police. They've come to pick you up."

We were taken in two cars, ours and a police vehicle, to the local police headquarters. There we were led to a room, and as usual, told to wait. This time, though, we were very well treated. We were asked what we wanted, if we needed anything for Anca. After lunch, which they served us there, Matei showed up. He was smiling and seemingly unaffected by everything that had happened.

After another hour of waiting, we were called to another office. A Romanian interpreter was present, who translated the police report of what had happened. It described the incident between Matei and the customs officer. The officer's statement was also read out; he admitted Matei had acted in self-defence, that his reaction was normal.

With those formalities completed, we were taken to a custodial house set aside for such cases, where we had to wait to be returned to Denmark, being the country we had come from.

We left everything in the car except for a few personal items, but these were also taken away from us at the detention centre. We were given two nicely furnished rooms, a living room with a TV, a kitchen and a bathroom. We had unrestricted access inside. But only Anca and I could go outside, and only for an hour, to a children's play area, and even here we were accompanied.

We were there for five days. We soon became restless, thinking they shouldn't keep us there so long if they were only going to return us to Denmark anyway. So we decided to go on hunger strike. Then we thought we needed to let people know what we were doing. Somehow we found some paper and glue, so we made and stuck notices to the windows. Only after we had already finished did we realise the windows all faced away from any streets or houses, so nobody would ever see them.

Although it was hard for me because I had to feed Anca, I joined in these little protests with the others. The guards looked unhappy about it, though we didn't see what harm it was causing them. It was not as if we had accomplished anything, but we couldn't sit still without doing something. Jean came to visit us. He confirmed what we were doing had caused some unhappiness amongst the border authorities, but he didn't say any more than that, and only left us more puzzled about how he knew this and what his motives were.

On the morning of the sixth day we were taken on the ferry back to Frederikshavn. We were put into a single cabin and five police officers were posted at the door. One of them was a woman and all of them seemed to be good at karate. Matei told me he had had a dream in which somebody pushed him hard in the shoulder. He said he could still feel the pain. We sat down, determined to wait calmly through the three-hour trip, even though we had nothing to do. But Anca was hungry. We approached the guards, who told us to wait. After half an hour, during which we waited calmly, Anca started to cry. We were escorted to the toilet although we didn't see where we could have escaped to, being in the middle of the North Sea. We asked the guards what was happening with Anca's food.

"Wait," was the response. Angrily, Matei approached one of them and asked how long it took just to get some chips. He found himself gripped by the shoulder, and when he tried to step back, the hold grew even stronger. The other guards stepped in, and after a short conversation among them, the female officer left and in a short time returned with the fries.

Ashore, we were surrendered to the Danish police. We were again put in cars, one of them being ours, and again we stopped at police headquarters. They gave us our car keys so we could get anything we wanted from the luggage, and then we were separated. This time things moved very quickly. We didn't know where Dragos and Matei were to be taken, but Carmen, Anca and I were led to a hotel and placed in the landlady's care.

We had the freedom to go anywhere outside the hotel. "Please don't try to escape," we were asked. Why would we when it was so comfortable here! We had everything we needed, including our meals at the hotel restaurant. We wanted to stay in Denmark. We didn't have a car, we didn't have money, and we were alone. I assured them that flight was the furthest thing from our minds.

Although we could go out whenever we wanted, it was still hard to fill the time, especially for Anca. Once again, Carmen and I went through all our childhood stories and songs, trying to give Anca a sense of security and trust. But all of us looked forward the most to mealtimes, when we could sit in the restaurant, with others around us, like normal people. We tried to make our meals last as long as possible.

Five days after we arrived, two policemen came and invited us to pack up everything we had. It was time to go, they said. Outside, looking very happy, Matei and Dragos were waiting for us.

"How come you're looking so happy? Did you enjoy where you were staying?" I asked.

"Looks like you were luckier than we were there," Matei said. "No, the reason we're so happy is that we have been accepted by Denmark! We're being taken to a refugee camp."

13

FINALLY SOME GOOD NEWS! AT LAST IT LOOKED AS IF WE might be on a path that had a future. Looking more closely now, I noticed how pale Dragos was. He had lost a lot of weight. It turned out that he had again gone on hunger strike and had even tried to cut his veins as a sign of protest at his recent incarceration. By good luck a warder had noticed in time and he was kept under observation for two days. Matei, by contrast, had worked in an electrical assembly shop. He'd even been paid.

We were allowed to travel alone in our car, following two policemen in their car to the camp. It was remarkable how completely this restored our dignity.

We were heading for Copenhagen. We crossed the sea to Odense Island, then on to Copenhagen Island where our camp was located. From the behaviour of our two escorts we could see that our status had changed, and for the better. We were treated with respect and kindness, and we felt the kind of freedom we had lost since leaving France. We could take walks at will, we were offered food, drinks, anything we wanted. We found it all quite hard to believe. We felt we had regained a sense of dignity.

The camp, called Sandholm, turned out to be the same place where Carmen, Anca and I had been locked up for four days on our first foray into Denmark. This time, though, we were on the other side of the wire fence, where we had so longed to be.

We were given ID cards, new bedsheets, towels, soap, pillows, toothbrushes, and had the use of bathrooms with toilets. In a few days, we were told, we could report to the camp warehouse to choose clothing for Anca. We met the Romanian interpreter, through whom we communicated with Danish officials during the entire time we stayed there.

An adjustment period followed, during which we tried to learn as much as possible about camp life. We met Doina and Cătălin, two young Romanians with whom we would stay in touch for years to come. They had arrived at the camp a few months before us, and shared with us their treasure trove of knowledge regarding camp life and the Danish immigration system.

We soon noticed throngs of people at the phones near the front gate of the camp. Cătălin revealed that somebody had discovered a code which you could use to call anywhere in the world without charge. We didn't let such an opportunity go to waste; from then on we were in constant contact with Remus, with Matei's parents and even with Jean, who promised to come to visit.

By now we had very little money, and while our meals, accommodation and all the incidentals were provided for, our goal was to leave for one of the countries that were still taking in immigrants. To do that we needed money. We couldn't save anything unless we could get placed in a camp where you got an allowance to prepare your own meals. Dragos appealed to the camp leadership to be transferred to such a place. He had suffered from hepatitis, he told them, and needed a special diet. We were put on a waiting list, but the chance was there, and at the end of each month we would ask whether any vacancies had come up.

From our perspective, being accepted as refugees meant we now had not just an improved quality of life, but an official status. Some people still looked down on us, however, or took whatever chance they could to let us know we were somehow lesser human beings. It was our extended family member – our much-loved Opel Senator – that was the next object of such behaviour.

Along with other car owners, we had parked our Opel outside the camp. But for some reason it aroused the ill will of one of the check-in guards at the gate.

"Where did you get this car from?" he started with, followed by, "How much did you pay?" and "Where did you get the money from?"

At first we answered politely, although it was none of his business. But he persisted. When we could see he was deliberately trying to intimidate and annoy us, we parked the car in a more remote area. Perhaps, we reasoned, he was behaving this way because he couldn't stand the thought that some down-on-their-luck immigrants could afford such a nice car. We thought that if he couldn't see it, he would leave it alone.

"Where is your car?" he asked us one morning. We told him we'd left it with a friend. But to our astonishment we saw him following us in his car as we walked to our new parking spot. We changed our direction, and after a while he turned back.

The next day we asked for a meeting with the camp director, at which, with the help of the interpreter, we complained about the guard's attitude and behaviour. It was all too close a reminder of life under a communist regime, where people with authority thought they could act as they pleased. We weren't told of the full outcome of our complaint, but we never saw that officer again.

We got a small weekly allowance, from which we tried to

update our wardrobe. That sounds somewhat pretentious, but after so long on the road, we were all in desperate need of new clothes and footwear. I had been wearing the skirt I got from Tina since leaving France, and a pair of her old shoes as well. Now I wore cheap tennis shoes and, in the changeable spring weather, I would often find myself standing in the puddle that formed in the centre of the phone booth where we made our phone calls. But I was less focused on my own health than on Anca's, and Matei too lacked many things.

Although it was unfortunate, it was our health that eventually supported our case for a spot in another camp. Anca caught a pulmonary infection that kept us on edge for a month and a half. Antibiotics were prescribed only in serious cases, and until one of the doctors realised that Anca's case was serious, it was a nightmare. The poor girl couldn't sleep for nights because of her coughing, and of course it kept us up as well. We insisted to the camp leadership that we needed to move out of our communal accommodation, and they promised it would happen soon.

In the meantime we took advantage of the freedom we had to get to know more about this wonderful country that had taken us in and where we had met such kind people. We explored the camp's surroundings. It was spring and everything was bursting with life; green fields, gardens filling with colour, impeccably kept farms; everything seemed inviting and spoke to us of the Danish people's industry and gentleness, qualities we were to discover in the people themselves.

We walked everywhere, saving up the bus tickets we were allocated every week for longer trips when we could take them. Cătălin and Doina accompanied us everywhere. For Anca's birthday, we put our roaming to good use. We found a nice sunny meadow where we could spend the day, surrounded by flowers and pine trees. We had nuts, beer and a layer cake large enough to accommodate four little candles.

"You know," Doina told us, "on the first day you appeared on the path in front of the bedrooms, we watched you from our window. You were all laughing, commenting on everything out loud and smiling. We said to ourselves, 'This is a titmice band; if you strike one, they all cry out'." It was pleasing to hear this Romanian saying, about the close-knit nature of the titmouse bird, made about our family. It made us like this couple all the more.

But this observation about our family also made me a little sad, for the other change happening at this time was the deterioration in the relationship between Matei and me. Before I really understood what was happening, we were fighting regularly. Each heated discussion resulted in hurtful words being directed at Dragos and me. An absurd jealousy about his position in the family was eating at Matei and he piled on me all the venom generated by a sick imagination. While everyone in the group participated in making our major decisions, it was true that most of the ideas we followed came from Dragos. But this was because his ideas were often the most reasonable and usually proved fruitful.

"Why?" Matei asked. "For once why don't you say, '*No*' and support my ideas?"

It was absurd to say no to something I could clearly see would work, I told him. I put up with Matei's abuse, believing that in order to succeed we needed harmony between us. But it hurt to know that his accusations could be heard in neighbouring apartments, leaving no doubt as to what was going on between us. Matei got angry with me over Dragos, and I got angry with him because he would spend so much of the little money we had on alcohol.

"You love him too much," he often said about Dragos, but no matter how hard I tried to demonstrate to him how wrong he was, he wouldn't listen. I became increasingly frustrated because Matei didn't seem to understand that now was the time to fight together for our common cause, not to fight each other. Only by standing together did we have any chance of success. I fought to maintain unity, but the price I was paying was becoming heavier and heavier.

There were some good days, but they were fewer and fewer, and I also worried about the impact of our fights on my daughter.

When Anca got stronger, she resumed her habit of bringing our breakfast from the cafeteria; she liked to arrange the milk, bread, butter and jam in a net bag and then proudly appear on the path between the cafeteria and the bedrooms. One morning, though, I heard her screaming and crying. She had tried to bring coffee as well, but the cup was too heavy and she had spilt it on her hand and scalded it. It was only a minor burn, however, and was treated successfully.

The camp was located near Blovstrod, a small, smart settlement not far from Copenhagen. I would walk in that direction most mornings and evenings, and one Saturday, out walking in the fresh morning air, I noticed large baskets of bottles, and others with clothing, in front of many houses. I remembered being told that on the first Saturday of each month, people would put out excess items for collection. I didn't waste a moment. I turned back to get the family and the car – I knew I couldn't manage this by myself. I'd heard there was a return fee paid for bottles, and I saw hundreds of kroner in the piles of bottles along the streets. We filled the trunk, picturing ourselves with the money we thought the bottles were worth, and grabbed a few items of clothing as well. We headed to a store and set the bottles on the counter, then waited.

"Was there something else?" asked the cashier.

"No, just the money for the bottles, please." we answered.

"They're of no value. But thank you for bringing them in."

It was a crushing disappointment, but it soon turned into a cause for much laughter.

Jean visited in summer, and brought with him the possibility of emigrating to New Zealand. Following a meeting at the New Zealand embassy in Brussels, he believed that since I was not officially married to Matei, the surest and quickest way to achieve residency would be a marriage of convenience – between himself and me. He was a citizen of New Zealand and thought that everything would go smoothly, and that it would possibly work for my sons as well. As for Matei, the idea was that Jean would make a formal invitation to him, and once he got there we could all sort ourselves out pretty easily.

I didn't have the slightest idea about immigration procedures, or Jean's motives, so I took his proposition at face value. It did seem to be to everyone's advantage; Jean wanted to escape loneliness and we needed a country to call our own. We had no one else stepping up to help us, so couldn't see how we could achieve anything without him.

About two months after we arrived at the camp, the phone company fixed the free-calling fault. We desperately looked for another way to communicate with Jean and also with Matei's parents that wouldn't cost money. We learned that private phone jacks were starting to be used, to hook into phone connections located on the outside wall of many buildings. The jacks and handsets were being rented out amongst those in the know in the camp. One Friday evening I was in the laundry room when Dragos appeared, seemingly in a very good mood.

"I talked with the Yugoslav," he told me, "he gave me a jack point, not far from here, and a phone. Let's go and speak with Jean and back home." I was desperate for such a chance, but unhappy Dragos had accepted something from a man who had a shady reputation around the camp. I told Dragos, but couldn't convince him to change his mind.

"What he does is his business. He gave me a spot, I paid and I want to try it out."

The spot was a sports hall not far from the camp. Though it was surrounded by a high wire fence, we found its gates wide open, as if we were expected. While Dragos made the preparations to install the phone, I heard a rustle in the woods on the other side of the fence.

"Dragos!" I said. "Someone's there. I don't understand how you could trust that man."

"You're always scared. There's nobody there."

I didn't say any more but I was surprised by his lack of caution, because he was normally extremely careful in such circumstances. Then I realised the problem. Dragos had been drinking with the Yugoslav, and that had made him more careless than usual.

Dragos connected the call, but I only managed to say "Hello," when headlights showed up through the gates.

"Quick, Dragos," I hissed at him. "Throw away the phone. It can only be the police."

Dragos took the phone and started to run towards the back of the building.

"Run, Mum! Hurry, keep up," he yelled.

"Throw that phone away!" He barely had time to throw it into a bush before I felt the light from the headlights fix on us.

"Don't stop, Mum, hurry up. I know there's a hole in the fence somewhere around here." I didn't know if he was telling the truth, or just being hopeful.

The car stopped, but we didn't. They had nothing to lose, knowing there was no escape. This told me a lot about the chance of there being a hole in the fence.

Dragos kept urging me on, but it wasn't easy for me. That same morning I had bought, along with some pants, a pair of mules that were not suitable at all for running. I didn't think to take them off. Even if I had I couldn't keep up with Dragos. He ran like the twenty-five-year-old he was, I like the forty-four-year-old I was. And so I stopped.

The car came to a stop and two men got out of it: one in police uniform and another in plain clothes. They spoke to me in Danish; scared as I was, I understood what they were asking me. They wanted to know where was the man I had been using the phone with. I had been right. The jack had been used for a long time; somebody had realised what was going on and decided to set a trap. Most probably, the Yugoslav had set Dragos up, getting one more fee and getting rid of the equipment at the same time. I kept silent while the men headed to the corner of the building where the phone connection was. I didn't think there was any escape for me and surprised myself by saying loudly and desperately, "God, please help me, save me."

I looked to the gate, and as if I had been pushed, began walking towards it without looking back. Any second I expected to be called back. But by a miracle I reached the highway unnoticed. I began looking around for a place I could hide. I went to the left of the highway, jumped over a ditch and started to climb a small hill covered in bush. Soon I came to a pleasant orchard, with the grass looking freshly cut in the moonlight. I couldn't calm down, and, still trying to work out where I was, began walking parallel to the road, thinking that at least this would take me closer to the camp.

I ran barefoot in the damp grass hoping to find a way out of the orchard when suddenly a living, thorny wall rose in front of me. It reminded me of my childhood fairy tales in which Ileana Cosânzeana and Prince Charming, in order to escape Baba Cloanța's tireless pursuit, threw a magic comb that turned into a wall very much like the one in front of me, to try to stop her. That didn't work in the story, but what was I to do now? I didn't have anything on me that could have helped. The fear that somebody could be following my tracks forced me on, but after a few steps the wall had become so thick any progress was impossible. I retreated, and this time, looking around, noticed a fence extending from the thick vegetation. I ran alongside it and came at last to a gate. It was locked, but beneath it was a small depression, like the ones made by naughty dogs sneaking out of their yards. I squeezed underneath and found myself in a well-tended house-garden, full of flowers and greenery. I crossed the garden and stole softly alongside the house. Dogs began barking inside, so I hurried out the front. To my joy I recognised the place as the area where we usually parked the car.

I just had to cross the road and I would have been at the front gates of the camp, but now I remembered that Dragos had my ID card, and there was no way I could get in without it. By now it must have been well past midnight. I knew there was a path going around the camp but I had never had the curiosity to follow it. I certainly never thought I would be exploring it in the middle of the night. It wasn't hard to find and soon I was walking alongside the fence towards the building where Dragos's apartment was. I grabbed a handful of small stones and started to throw them at the windows, trying to get somebody to come out. Soon a familiar face appeared at the window, one of Dragos's neighbours. I signalled desperately to him, trying to get him to come outside. Eventually he disappeared and came down. He was Russian and though neither of us spoke each other's language, he soon understood me. I suppose the circumstances helped, for he hurried back into the building, and at last, Dragos appeared, clean, wearing fresh clothes and seeming like he had just woken up.

"What is it, Mum? What are you doing here?"

"What are you saying?" I asked him.

"I am asking you what you are doing here, at this time of the night."

"Dragos, what's wrong with you? You know what I'm doing here. Now hurry up and give me my card."

"What card?"

I couldn't believe what I was hearing. "Dragos, have you gone mad? Snap out of it and stop torturing me. How can you ask me what I'm doing here? I've come from the phone jack, that's where. Now give me my card."

Lowering his voice, he said, "Mum, don't be upset. I thought they'd caught you and brought you here as a decoy."

"Oh, for heaven's sake! If they'd caught me, they would have brought me through the main gate in a car, and I wouldn't be here begging you to give me my card."

At last he had the decency to look a little sheepish. "I'm sorry, Mum. I haven't got any cards. I threw them in a bush in the forest."

"What? Why would you do such a thing? Tell me, what am I going to do now? How did you get in?"

"I jumped the fence." He looked up, then back at me: "I think you might have to, too." The fence was very high, as if for a prison, and it had three rows of barbed wire running along the top.

"Get Matei," I told him. Dragos returned with Matei, but I could see he was drunk again, and it made me more upset than ever to see him like that at a time when I really needed him. Both he and Dragos settled into a catching position. I threw my mules over and started to climb. Eventually, with my new pants considerably worse for the journey, I landed on the other side and we headed towards Dragos's room, where Carmen hid all the evidence in the garbage basket.

I didn't stay to listen to Dragos's story. I was still filled with fear at what we had done, and how close we had come to being caught, and that we had been followed. I had a sleepless night. All my life I had never been in trouble with the authorities and now I felt uneasy that during such a short period of time I had so frequently crossed paths with the police.

Next morning at six, Dragos knocked on our door, and he and Matei set out to retrieve the phone and our precious blue cards. They came back about two hours later with both. At last we felt we could relax a little, and I could calmly listen to Dragos's adventure last night. After passing through the hole in the fence, he headed deeper into the forest. Then, hearing dogs in the distance, he was convinced they were on his scent, so he ran and ran without stopping. As he ran, he threw away the cards and kept right on running until he realised at last that it was quiet around him. At first he thought of going to Kalundborg, the new camp where Cătălin and Doina now lived. But he remembered the time, and that he didn't have any way of getting there, and that he now had no ID, so he decided to jump the fence back into our camp.

That was the last time we tried to make any cheap long-distance calls, and the last time we had anything to do with the Yugoslav.

14

Food in the camp was not at all bad, but if you got to the cafeteria late, all the salad looked as if a few hens had dug through it. So we were careful to be among the first to arrive whenever we could. Some days they served delicacies such as turkey breast, chicken thighs or feta cheese, that we absolutely loved. One time, before Cătălin and Doina had left, we heard that roast chicken would be served, but when we arrived early, we found they were still serving the fish pie left over from the previous evening. Dragos went to the kitchen to ask whether it was true, that there was roast chicken. He soon returned, looking confused.

"I don't know what's going on. I asked whether they were going to have 'kitchen' and everybody started to laugh; something seemed to amuse them. Then they asked what I wanted and I said very clearly 'kitchen'. But they wouldn't stop laughing and so I left."

"What did you say you asked for?" Cătălin asked.

Before he could answer, Dragos smiled, then laughed. "Okay, now I get why they were amused."

It didn't look as if the fish would be finished any time soon. Now Cătălin had an idea, "Let's fill plates with fish pie and stack them in the box by the kitchen." Somebody noticed what we were doing, and asked us whether we liked fish that much. "Oh, yes, very much." Cătălin answered. "And we're three families together, so we eat quite a lot. It's very tasty."

We managed to empty the fish trays, and were rewarded with a plate of chicken which we took back to our rooms. They were small victories, these childish endeavours, but how much we needed them at the time.

A short time later Cătălin and Doina moved out. We missed them and visited them almost every week, until we decided to sell our car. That, too, saddened us as if we had lost a good friend.

Denmark represented a launching pad for us, from where we would eventually land in another place, but we still could not see how we could achieve this without Jean. We hoped for his help, but we knew we had to see him to prod him into action. So we decided to cross into Sweden, to visit him in his place in Göteborg.

We knew there were small ferries that made daily runs between the two countries, and that the closest border point was Helsingor. One Sunday morning, Dragos and I boarded a ferry as it was preparing to leave. We could hardly relate to our fellow passengers, who seemed so relaxed; they ate, drank and sang while we were tense with worry over whether we would be stopped by immigration officers. It was a short crossing, and the ship soon tied up at the quay at Göteborg. We wandered slowly off the boat, expecting others to join us, but then saw that almost everyone seemed to be staying where they were. We realised they must have been on some kind of a pleasure trip, on board just as a different place to have their morning coffee.

"Passport please," I heard someone say. While we had been figuring out what was going on, without realizing it we had arrived in front of the immigration officers. I saw Dragos turn red, but with a composure that I had always admired in him, he answered calmly, "My wife has them, she will be here any second."

Scared, I looked behind me. I couldn't see anyone else. I was the last one nearing the checkpoint. Immediately both of us did an about-turn and walked quickly back towards the ship. My legs were rigid, trembling, and I was afraid to look back for fear of seeing the officers following us. As we neared the ship we got our courage up and ran the last few metres. We both heaved sighs of relief, as if we had escaped a great danger, but we didn't really feel safe until we felt the ship moving.

We couldn't give up our quest though. Somehow we had to reach Sweden. A few days later we left Anca in the care of some housemates and headed to the same place, with a different plan. This time we would rent a boat and pretend we were going fishing. We fitted ourselves out with the necessary equipment and estimated the distance between the two shores.

"It's not far – just a stone's throw," we told each other, and climbed purposefully into the little boat. We put on our life jackets, the owner wished us good fishing, and, squeezing through the numerous ships in the harbour, we headed out to sea. I sat at the prow, Matei at the rudder and Dragos and Carmen "fished". We slowly got farther and farther away from shore, until suddenly there was nothing around us but water. The waves seemed to grow larger and larger by the second. Gripped by fear, I said, "Take me back now or I'll scream. If you want to go to Sweden this way, then that's your business."

I expected some objections, but to my surprise I didn't hear one. Just the opposite: very quickly we changed direction, and I realised that none of us was at all confident. When we were close to shore we stopped again to "fish". Matei tried to keep the boat in position, but being clumsy and anxious, when one of the two "fishermen" cried, "Left!" he turned right and vice-versa, so that at one stage we were going round and round in circles of various circumferences. Finally, someone said, "We're wasting our time. Let's go home."

When we returned the boat, the owner asked us if we'd had any problems. The coastguard had called him to ask if he knew what was going on with his boat, because it seemed to be in some distress.

From what we heard in the camp, we understood that unless something unexpected happened, we would be staying in Denmark for about two years before we could expect to be accepted by a third country. If that was the case, we had a lot of time we could take advantage of. We were not tramps, content with or resigned to living an unsettled existence. We had to do something with a view to improving our chances of successfully emigrating to a stable destination.

The question was, what could we do?

Just when we needed to be calm in our souls and in our minds, to help us cope with our state of uncertainty, our failed attempts to visit Jean became another sore point between Matei and me. We wound up going over the same never-ending discussions about what we could do, and what options we had. The thought that we had asked for Jean's help, and tried to reach out to him, made Matei deeply unhappy.

To make matters worse, each time we called Jean in Sweden, it seemed like he was backing away from his promises to help us.

"I'm ready to try anything if you've got any better ideas," I told Matei. I wasn't happy with what we'd done or the situation we were in either, but I couldn't see any other option. People talked a lot about the chances and requirements of emigrating to Canada or

Australia, but I had passed the age of forty and Matei didn't have any of the priority skills for those countries. So it seemed we had little option but to pin our hopes on Jean's promises, and this feeling of our future being out of our control only made things worse.

The tension between us grew. I was angry every day, and so was Matei. I could understand his point of view, but I couldn't accept the harsh and hurtful words that rolled off his tongue. It was as though he wanted me to suffer more than I already was, knowing full well his habit of confessing to others and complaining that he wasn't understood. He gradually became more isolated, not wanting to participate in any plans or decisions that we made. Then he would blame me for keeping him on the sidelines, for not considering his opinions. It was hard for everyone. I am not a particularly tactful or patient person, and that was even more the case in those days. I needed someone to understand me and what I was going through just as much as Matei did.

We called Jean again. It wasn't acceptable, we said, it was unfair, after giving us such hope, to renege on his promise to help. He couldn't or wouldn't give us any clear story why his stance had changed, faltering every time he tried to answer one of our questions. "This is cowardice," I finally told him, "You owe us a clear explanation, and if you don't want to provide it over the phone I will come to you." He promised then he would come, and this calmed us down a bit.

Ever since I was young, when I've been sad, I've sung. Over the years, that's changed – it's mostly crying now – but back then, joy as well as sorrow overflowed into song. I favoured nostalgic, romantic songs, that stirred in me hidden thoughts and longing, and moistened my eyes. But when I was happy I would turn to music from the inexhaustible river of beauty that is our folklore. I have collected music since my adolescence and always carried a songbook with me, full of the richness of our folklore. Later when I came into contact with people who didn't speak our language, I would try to translate verses or folk poems, to make them understand the genius of the Romanian people.

On good days Matei would accompany me on his harmonica, and when I was embittered with sorrow, I would ask in song, "Mother Fate, Mother Fate, what have you got against me? Why don't you let me live, live in this world?" or, in an appeal to one of the three spirits of Romanian folklore who predict the fates of the newborn, "'Tell me, *Ticuleana,* tell me if there is any luck left for me in this world?' 'The luck you had, you lost by your own doing. You passed by a puddle, your luck fell into the water'."

Sometimes I would think of my family, and sing their favourite songs, giving priority to my father who particularly liked the love song, "Beautiful Cart with Four Oxen." I longed for home, for the country people, for those places where I truly knew the Romanian soul: full of humour, optimistic even in poverty and adversity, eager to celebrate, sentimental but at the same time wise.

What a pity the misfortune called "Communism" settled in our country and tried to destroy our soul. I wasn't happy that I had left home, believing that everyone's place is where he or she was born. And I wasn't thinking that way just because we were in a precarious situation. It was because my soul was, is and will always be there – at home. Later, during my travels, I met many Romanians who had emigrated and who had an enviable financial situation, but I never believed them to be happy, never believed that they didn't think longingly of home, that they didn't crave the inner life which, no matter how hard we might strive, cannot be replaced by a good material situation.

Jean arrived, full of apologies for the "misunderstanding" that had come about. He promised to work with us on our case. We took heart somewhat, especially since soon after he left we were told that we would be moved to the Dianalund camp.

We were to live at Dianalund for a year and a half, in a residential block surrounded by an immense park full of greenery and flowers, with a forest just a short walk away, farms all around, stores, bus stops, everything we needed, even a church, all within easy reach. After everything we had been through, these simple facilities were heaven on earth for us. Even now, after so many years, I am filled with regret that we had to leave a place that was so good for my soul, despite the fear of deportation we lived with most of the time.

We were given a room where initially all five of us lived for a month. During this time Dragos and Carmen witnessed first-hand the state of things between me and Matei. And they were not the only ones, since the hallway on our floor had permanent traffic and the neighbours were mostly Romanian.

Dragos and Carmen then moved to a room on the ground floor, where the communal kitchen was. The laundry was in the basement, while on the floor above us were the most desirable apartments, with two rooms each.

I was usually the first one in the kitchen in the morning, wanting to get breakfast over with so I could spend the rest of the day as I wished. Most of our countrymen had arrived a year before we did and like us they were aware of the very slight chance we had of staying in Denmark. Most of them had filed papers to emigrate to Canada, some had taken the option of Australia. We were still thinking of New Zealand; the idea didn't cross our minds that we wouldn't get placed somewhere eventually.

As usual in a new place, over the first few days we gathered information. Most people used bicycles to go short distances, very few had cars and we started by finding our way around on foot. With Dragos I discovered a shortcut that led out of the compound, to the back entrances of the shops. There we noticed a lot of cases with fruit, especially grapes and bananas, stacked up by an immense garbage skip.

I asked Dragos what he thought of so many fruit cases being left near where, in my opinion, only spoiled merchandise should have been thrown.

"I don't know," he said. "Let's come back later, towards evening, and see what happens." When we returned, we found fewer cases outside, but out of curiosity we opened the lids of the garbage bin and saw that the others had been thrown in there, along with bags of sugar, flour and everything that can be found in a supermarket. We picked a few out and inspected them, trying to understand why they were in there. They were not out of date, as we had expected, but there were little tears in the packaging or a scratch here and there, that probably caused their removal from the store's shelves. We took everything we could carry home, and from then on, every night we went and took everything that was clean and well packaged; cases of tomatoes that seemed just picked, bananas, apples, pears, peppers, the whole range of vegetables. There really was everything you could find in a store. Soon finding ourselves over-stocked, we started to give things to the neighbours.

Then we began to notice that the goods weren't of the same quality as before. One evening Matei, Dragos and I left our building from a different exit, where we bumped into two of our neighbours, also Romanian. They were carrying cases full of various items from the bins. "Oh, so it was you," Matei said. "We should have known you weren't being open."

This wasn't the only time in our travels that made me ask myself why there seemed to be no honesty among Romanians abroad. Most of us had left the same sorry country for the same reasons. We shared the same deep heritage that I loved. I couldn't understand why, with only a very few exceptions, wherever I met Romanians, their relationships with others were filled with jealousy and fighting, and our exchanges were usually only barely cordial.

By now a lawyer had been assigned to our case. We visited Mr. Gabrielsen with a view to finding out how we could extend our stay as long as possible. Dragos and Carmen followed his advice, and the example of most of the other camp residents, and filed papers to emigrate to Canada. Matei and I had no chance there, however.

So we kept in touch with Jean, and it was at about this time he told me he had sent our immigration papers to Brussels and, at the same time, had asked for information from his ex-wife, in Wellington.

"What information?" I asked.

"She used to work for the immigration office and –".

"What did you tell her?"

"I told her we would enter into a marriage of convenience to facilitate your immigration."

I was astonished. "I don't want to hear about it. If that's your plan, we'll never get an immigration visa."

Jean tried to pacify me. "My ex-wife and I are friends, even though we divorced twenty-five years ago. You know, she once wrote to me that it would be good for us to get together again, on the grounds that most artists do that. But I told her I wasn't an actor."

He was joking, but it was also possible I had passed up a chance to move on. A thought came to me, "What if he had committed this indiscretion just to make me react harshly, so he could wash his hands of us?" I chased the thought away. I didn't want to believe somebody could be so heinous as to betray us while knowing our predicament.

I couldn't give up on Jean, so decided to make another attempt to get to Sweden, this time with Carmen. It wasn't hard for us to alter our looks to fit in a little better, and in an hour both of us were blonde and mentally prepared to cross the border in front of the customs officers but without passports. We mixed in with other passengers, and this time luck was on our side; half an hour after the ferry docked we were on the train to Göteborg.

We wanted to stay in close touch with Jean because by now I knew that if we didn't, he wouldn't make any effort on our behalf. We met at his house, and I suggested to him that before he went to New Zealand, as he said he intended to do, he would need to sort out the pension he was getting from Norway to make sure he would get it in New Zealand. He went to Norway and returned three days later, saying there was nothing to prevent him from leaving for New Zealand.

Back we went to Denmark, but two weeks later, Jean called saying he wanted someone to stay in his house while he went to Romania. It seemed important to keep up the relationship, so I crossed into Sweden again, this time with Anca. I covered her thick chestnut hair with a hat and told her to keep her head down. She did well, and on the train to Göteborg Anca told me, "You know, I have to tell you, I got a very good view of the immigration officer's shoes. I was very close to him."

We stayed for ten days without a word from Jean, so I decided to call one of his relatives, who told me Jean had been invited to stay with a woman he had once intended to marry. During the visit, one of his legs had swollen up, he couldn't move and he was now under medical care. It would be another two weeks before he would be able to come home. I decided to return to Denmark in the meantime, and come back just one or two days before Jean's arrival.

It was hard being alone in a strange place without being able to talk to anyone. I glanced through a few Romanian books, then I don't know whether it was weakness or curiosity that pushed me to do what I considered a sin, but I started to look through the bags of papers and photos that filled a considerable corner of one of the bedrooms.

I soon discovered what Teodor had suspected all those years ago: Jean had worked hand-in-hand with the Securitate, the Romanian secret police.

15

THE FOLLOWING LETTER CLEARED THINGS UP FOR ME considerably:

Esteemed Jean

I am a Romanian citizen settled abroad, like you. Recently, I rang home to find my relatives in good health. By chance I met your friend in Craiova, the security colonel with whom you spent many hours here in the country. He is back to his former trade and he wanted to unload his soul of many things. That's how he told me all the news you brought him about the Romanians in Sweden, phone numbers, addresses, activities, and thoughts. What were you doing in Sweden, esteemed Jean? Were you helping Ceaucescu to stay out of trouble? What did you plan to do with the dollars you got from Romania? You wanted to be in league with the priest and have the whole of Sweden in your hands? You didn't succeed, so out of fear, you returned the money.

What mission did you get next? To give money to a Jewish woman in order to learn what's going on in Paris. You were happy to succeed, and then you got your reward. Your grandchildren, relatives, they all came to see you when even birds were not allowed out of Romania.

I am staying here a bit longer. I promise to make a special trip to Göteborg to meet you and to help the Romanians there learn what you did, you and others who, for years, turned in honest people, who helped a dictator stay in power. Many things will be brought to light here in the country and spies have no business staying here. Our wretched relatives and those who fled in search of a free life have had enough.

Looking through the papers stashed in plastic bags, I found all of our documents from Norway, along with our pictures, and even the forms which Ion and I had filled in when trying to gain refugee status in Norway. Everything spun before my eyes. Now I could understand the significance of so many things that didn't make sense. Jean, a spy! It was true, and right now he was playing with us, with me.

He didn't really intend to do anything to help us. He just wanted to waste our time. It was me he wanted, but he didn't have the courage to actually try anything. I remembered on the first visit he paid us in Denmark, when I went to pick him up from his hotel in the morning, he had tried to kiss me. I pulled away and pretended to let it pass unnoticed. Then, in Sweden, he would half-joke that I should stay there with him, that "I will buy a beautiful house, I will do anything to make you feel good."

I hadn't listened, I'd just let everything pass without thinking about what was going on, being preoccupied with trying to resolve something for all of us who had left home together. In Norway he had fulfilled his mission, succeeding in persuading us to return.

Now what did he want? What should I do? Should I stay and confront him, or just leave? Despite the evidence, I still couldn't give up the notion that Jean had the power to help us. Yet no matter what lay behind the "help" he had offered to give, I could see clearly that any further meetings with him would be dangerous.

While still in his house waiting for his return I took a call from a man in New Zealand who was looking for Jean. He introduced himself as a friend and said his name was Mihai. From our conversation, I understood that he was aware of our situation, and said Jean had suggested he, Mihai, could help us immigrate to New Zealand.

"I have helped a lot of Romanians and I could do something for you as well," he said.

So, I thought, Jean wants to pass our case to this man.

Mihai asked for my phone number at the camp, saying he would call me there when I got back. A week later, Jean finally returned from Romania. He seemed very happy to find me in his house, but his smile disappeared when I showed him a phone bill for 12,000 kroners and asked him for another 6,000 for the immigration lawyer's fee, whom we had hired at his suggestion.

Then I gathered together all the papers referring to my stay in Norway, and threw them in his face.

"You low, miserable spy!"

"It's not nice to rummage through somebody else's papers."

It wasn't much of a rebuke, but I don't think I expected much more. "You're in no position to tell me what's nice and what isn't," I told him, "so don't try."

The next day I returned to Denmark, still angry, but with the money in my pocket. There I was met with the news that our application for New Zealand had been rejected. Looking back, and knowing what I had just learned about Jean, this should have come as no surprise. But rejection, like a slap in the face, still stings even when you are expecting it.

On the path in front of the camp I met Matei, pushing a stroller with a box full of wine in it.

"What are you doing? That must have cost a fortune," I said.

"I wanted to stock up. They were on sale, and as it's your name day and Anca's birthday in a few days, I thought it was a good idea. Hey, you just got back, don't get upset."

In the evening he got drunk and as usual, he felt like talking, but mostly arguing. Seeing that things were about to take a turn for the worse, I took advantage of a momentary lack of attention on his part and sneaked out. It was late, but the sky was clear and everything was lit by the rays of a gentle moon. I hid myself in the night, moving quickly from one place to another before settling behind a bush from where I could see Matei.

"Where did she disappear to...? I'll show you." I wasn't curious to find out what he wanted to show me, so I stayed hidden for an hour or more, until I thought that Matei would have fallen asleep.

The next day it was hard to look at him, so I left early on my bike, wishing to be alone, and hoping that a ride in the fresh morning air would help free me from the pain that was slowly and surely strangling me.

We celebrated Anca's birthday at the kindergarten where all the camp children had gathered. Before lunch Matei came to me with a bouquet of blue flowers. He told me he was sorry, and I knew he was, but it was hard to live when the days were mostly bad rather than good. For now, however, I didn't want to be angry, and I remembered a song which he liked me to sing for him: "Please, have patience with me and believe me, believe me that I love you."

Jean wrote to me, suggesting openly for the first time that Anca and I move to Sweden. "I will do anything, etc." It seemed quite mad, what he was suggesting, but it was clear he didn't want me to make his story public, knowing that I had taken all those compromising letters with me. I didn't reply.

Not long afterwards, Mihai called me. Then, and at other times, I was impressed by the length of the calls, and his invitation to, "Call any time, at any hour, collect." I wondered what the meaning of this could be, but it sounded great.

I should explain how I had come to ride a bike, which was a skill I'd never learned as a girl. When we finally obtained rooms on the much-envied floor where the apartments had two rooms, we wanted to decorate them as nicely as we could. That meant a few trips to a second-hand store. We only needed bikes. One day I found an abandoned one that looked pretty good; it just needed new tires. Dragos sorted these out and set up the bike for me, but there was one problem: I had never in my life ridden a bike.

One nice summer day, Matei, Dragos and Carmen invited me to the front of the camp, saying there was a nice surprise awaiting me. But when I got there, they showed me the bicycle, surrounded me, and told me, "Now you learn."

An hour later I was happily riding around the camp on my bike, and from then on I don't think there was any road within a one or two hour radius that I didn't know. Green fertile fields extended everywhere; I knew all the surrounding farms, but also the farmers from whom I bought milk, cheese, meat, poultry, and vegetables, everything I needed. That bike brought me a lot of satisfaction, but my greatest joy was that I had the means of meeting people, to get to know them better, and find out what was hiding under the so-called "Nordic coldness". Being a blue-eyed blonde, they would greet me as a local, but even when they discovered the truth they would smile in a friendly manner and try to help me understand their good intentions.

Dragos and Carmen were waiting for their interview for

Canada, but Dragos kept hoping something would come up in which we would be included as well. Mihai called regularly but I didn't put much hope in his plans, thinking that it was too complicated and unlikely that all of us could leave for New Zealand at the same time.

With the exception of a family that had applied for Australia, the other Romanian families in the camp had been accepted for Canada. Only Matei, Anca and I, and one other family – Gelu, Tina and their two kids – got nowhere. Matei and Gelu had both gone to military school in Romania. They didn't even bother contacting any embassies anymore; they knew they would be rejected.

Some of our campmates suggested we ask the ex-Romanian king, who was now in exile, for help. He was related to the Queen of Denmark, and on another occasion in a similar case many years ago he had acted on behalf of a group of Romanian emigrants. Everybody agreed it was worth trying, so we did. We eventually received a polite response, to the effect that we, and Romanians everywhere, were encouraged to return home and put our shoulders to the tasks of rebuilding the nation and helping Romania integrate with other civilized nations.

We decided to try to contact some other embassies, beginning with Indonesia. They would accept us, they said, but there was a year-long waiting period and we were not certain we would be staying where we were for that long.

Next was Ireland. It was possible, but we knew there was trouble there and we didn't need anything like that. So we knocked at the gate of Israel's embassy. By intercom we were asked what we wanted. "We want to emigrate to Israel."

The gate was opened, and it closed behind us equally quickly. A voice told us to empty our pockets and then it continued, "Where are you coming from? Who sent you?" We answered honestly and were taken to an office where we had a short conversation with an embassy clerk.

"What do you want to do in Israel?"

"Work, live, maybe do some business, we don't know exactly yet."

To this, he smilingly replied, "Then, why not go to America?" But proceeded to ask, "What is your religion?"

"Orthodox Christian." We asked him whether he thought we had a chance of emigrating to Israel.

"It would be difficult. Very difficult."

With another group of enthusiasts, we decided to take a trip to the U.S. Embassy. The group's spokesperson was Irina, our neighbour from the first camp. She was the only person I have met from Romania whose soul and intellectual quality made me trust her immediately. She had also crossed illegally into Denmark after staying for a while in Germany with her two sons, four and six years old. She spoke fluent French and English and so was unanimously chosen to represent our interests. As expected, she made a good impression on the two representatives of the Embassy but, with honest regrets, they were unable to help us.

We thought again of Israel. Maybe if we converted to Judaism, we could improve our chances. It was worth finding out a bit more, we felt, so we left for Copenhagen to find a rabbi.

It sounds farfetched and naïve, I suppose, but when you are desperately looking for something, you knock on every door, hoping that it will open for you and you will find what you desire.

We didn't know any rabbis, so we knocked on a few doors near a synagogue, and by chance met someone who set up a meeting for us at his house. Soon we were sitting with a man rich in years and refinement, his face stamped with intelligence, who listened to our story. Gently and attentively, he encouraged us to unveil our intentions, making us feel very relaxed and trustful. He asked us a series of questions and everything we had to say was relayed to him through Carmen. We talked openly, explaining what we wanted to do, this being, in our opinion, our only chance to emigrate.

I was pleasantly surprised when Carmen told me, "The Rabbi asks me to tell you that he likes your temperament." I thanked him and expressed my regret that I didn't speak English, thus missing this rare occasion to communicate with such a personality. He laughed, saying, "I also regret I don't speak Romanian."

Finally, he gave us his thoughts. "Listen. I am an old man, and I am going to give you an honest piece of advice from the bottom of my heart. Don't do this! I am convinced you will find a way, something to take you to what you want. You are going to succeed, believe me. I don't know how, because if I did I would tell you. But you will succeed."

I have never forgotten how solemnly he made this pronouncement. It wasn't the outcome we were hoping for, if we even were hoping for something. But it was valuable encouragement, and that was important after living so long with an uncertain future.

Shortly after our talk with the rabbi we received a message which, while it wasn't exactly divine intervention, turned out to be almost as good. Mr. Gabrielsen wanted to see us – all of us. It meant another train journey to Arhus, but the trip didn't cost us anything and he was a pleasant man, elegant in his speech and behaviour, who genuinely wanted to help us. We were curious to know what he wanted to say.

It turned out that he had been approached by the largest daily paper in Copenhagen, which was planning a feature on the refugee situation in Denmark. Did we want to be featured in the story?

We felt we had nothing to lose, so in a few days we were sitting at a table in the newspaper offices with a journalist, who wanted to know as many details as possible about our journey, from the time we left home to now. We were served lunch, and then we were taken to a park where they took a picture of us. In a few days, this picture appeared on the front page of the newspaper, with an article headlined, "With Anca In A Backpack." It summarised our recent travels and the situation we were currently in.

The publicity worked. Although they had been the last to file for immigration to Canada, Dragos and Carmen were the first ones called for an interview. Their anxiety was indescribable, but they returned happy – they had been granted permission to emigrate to Canada. They were to leave the camp within a month or two.

Their joy was great, but it didn't last long. A week before they were to leave, they received an order for deportation to Romania. Luckily Dragos had been as organised as usual: immediately after the successful interview, he and Carmen had sent all their belongings to Canada, in care of another family that had left not long before. With only their hand luggage, they were able to hide out with some friends in Dianalund and avoid the deportation officials.

Usually when you got your visa or were about to get it, the police agreed to extend permission to stay in Denmark until the departure date, and they would even pay for the plane tickets. We didn't know why, but this hadn't applied in Dragos and Carmen's case. I told Mr. Gabrielsen, who was able to get them permission to stay for a few days longer. But they remained in hiding, and bought their own plane tickets. They had checked the flight times and found that the flight the police were going to put them on left at the same time as another one – to Romania.

And then they were gone. Finally, after so much shared hope and trial, failures and successes, we were no longer together. I was heartbroken. I felt all my hopes had left with the one man I could really confer with and trust – Dragos. I was glad they had got away, of course, but when I went into their room, that not long before had been full of our laughter and noise, and was now empty, I sat in the middle of the floor and sobbed.

Someone knocked on the door, and the camp director entered, accompanied by two policemen. They asked where Dragos was.

"They've gone. To Canada."

"But we have their plane tickets."

"Their plane's gone." I told them. "They didn't trust you. They were afraid you'd deport them, so they paid for their own tickets, even though they'll reach Canada with only $50 in their pocket."

A few weeks later we got an audiocassette from Dragos and Carmen. They described in the minutest details their first impressions of their new country, and their plans for the near future. They were happy. For them, the future was at last full of promise.

16

MATEI, ANCA AND I WERE ALONE. I TOOK NO PLEASURE FROM anything anymore, and nothing seemed worth starting. Before he left, Dragos used to come into the kitchen every morning knowing I would be there and together we would plan the day. Now, as I poked listlessly at whatever I was trying to do, I would turn in hope at every noise, expecting to see him and his smiling, trusting face.

Just two other Romanian families were left in the camp: Fanel and Jeni were also waiting to leave for Canada. Gelu and Tina, whom I mentioned earlier, had made a lot of friends among the Danes and had been given a lot of promises. They were hoping one would come through and they'd be able to stay. "What do we do?" we asked ourselves. I was still thinking of New Zealand. Deep in my soul, I knew my future didn't include Matei, but I couldn't leave without knowing how his situation would be resolved. Then one evening, Matei had an idea.

"Why don't I apply using my high school diploma? Instead of

my army background? It shows a specialisation in building and electrical work.

"That's a good idea," I said. "But you've never done any work in those fields."

"True. That's why I haven't had the courage to try it before. But now I think I will."

We headed for the Australian Embassy, where, through the goodwill of one of the women there, we got the list of priority trades. Electricians were at the top of the list. I met the points required for immigration, under trades and skills, but earned none under the age criterion, since I was over forty. Matei, however, had a chance. The only problem was that Anca and I had to accompany him; being with his family, he would have a better chance. Of course we would do that. We would go together to Australia, and from there I could leave for New Zealand.

Mihai, in New Zealand, was calling more and more frequently. Since his calls lasted for at least an hour, sometimes even two or three, I had to give him the number of a phone booth across from the camp, where he would call me at certain pre-arranged times. He told stories from his youth, about his family, his immigration to New Zealand, his former wife, his children and so much more. I asked myself how he could pay for these calls, which must have cost him over $1,000 a month – at one time he told me he even had to pay $3,000.

He told me he was known by the nickname Mişu, and I asked myself what kind of man this "Mişu" could be if, as Jean had said, he had been a spy for the first communist regime in our country and had betrayed his masters to leave for New Zealand? These alarm signals didn't stop me however, since the most important thing for me was to get out of there, and in my situation everything he said sounded tempting and reasonable.

"I will help you bring your children over so that you have them near you ... I have two houses ... My company brings in money ... I have helped so many, and so in my old age I cannot do otherwise, especially since you are from my own country ... I understand your other son is finishing his university studies. Why doesn't he come here?" These were the words I heard, the promises I thought were being made. When he talked about sending Anca to a private school, I thought I just couldn't ignore them any longer.

But then I would ask myself whether under normal circumstances I would have believed everything this man was saying.

"Maybe not, but for now I am okay."

I'd breathe out a sigh, then tell myself that to have Remus with me as well was a dream that I could scarcely believe. But I was still willing to try for it. I wrote to Remus. He had a new girlfriend, who strongly wanted to leave the country, and they would make their decision on whether or not to leave after his final exam.

But while Mişu was good at telling me what I wanted to hear, he dragged his feet when it came to getting anything done. A year had passed, and he hadn't achieved anything for real. Again, I didn't really stop to ponder this, and what it meant. Then he let me know he had found a very good lawyer who only dealt with immigration issues, from whom he'd learned that the reason things were going nowhere was that Jean's ex-wife had written to the immigration office in Brussels, revealing my intention to enter a marriage of convenience with Jean; so there was now a black spot on my immigration file. I had suspected this, but what could I do? I wouldn't receive any news from Australia for at least three months, and I didn't even know whether it would be good or bad.

Matei was very upset that I had decided we should go our separate ways, but I assured him that in order to help him, regardless of how things developed, first I would leave with him for Australia. And if the news regarding his immigration there wasn't good, I wouldn't go on to New Zealand until I knew he was on a safe track.

I had become friends with Jeni and Fanel by now, and as Fanel was an auto electrician, he had started to help Matei refresh and update his knowledge of the trade. In Jeni I found a true friend: delicate, sensitive, and very tactful. She was a great help to me during those days, as things were getting worse and worse with Matei. He wandered from one place to the next without my knowing much about what he did, and he always stank of booze and was in a fighting mood. Another source of strength for me was the Middle Eastern couple that I had noticed when we first arrived. Naser and Kaiwan had recently moved to the same floor as us, and also became my good and steadfast friends. Naser was a handsome, well-educated Iraqi, and Kaiwan was from Iran. Before she had come to Denmark, Kaiwan had worked in Romania for four or five months, and this helped us understand each other.

Matei came back after a weekend away, saying he had been to Sandholm, the first camp where we had lived, to meet a former acquaintance from Romania. She had come there at his request, and he said he wanted to take her with him to Australia.

"You know you can only leave with me and Anca," I told him. "Why do you mislead people?" He answered me with unrepeatable words.

One morning, after he had been gone the whole night, he came home, showered, then fell into bed. I was at the table with Anca and not in a good mood. The smell of tobacco mixed with booze made things worse – it always gave me a feeling of moral decadence that made me feel humiliated and insulted. Anca, sensing that something wasn't right, didn't want to eat and started to moan. I pushed her plate in front of her, harder than I should have, and everything went tumbling onto the floor. Before I could do anything, Matei, who seemed to have been waiting for just such an excuse, came up behind me and began hitting me viciously. I didn't know what was going on, and under the rain of blows I couldn't open my mouth to ask. I tried to flee to Anca's and my room, because I didn't want anybody in the hallway to overhear us, but he followed me, and his fists landed with unchecked fury all over my body. His main target however was my head.

"I don't want my wife to be smarter than me," he screamed. "I'll show you how smart you are. You think you're so good. So what?"

I was afraid for my life, he was so angry. Fortunately Anca escaped out the front door, and before long Naser showed up with the camp director. The beating stopped.

"It's my business," Matei said stiffly to the two men. "She is my wife, this is my place and I gave her what she deserved." At that moment, I hated him; I hated him with all my being for the humiliation he exposed me to.

From then on Naser avoided Matei and never talked to him again until he left the camp. Later, he told me that Anca had run to him and, crying, told him what was going on in our room.

Of course, everybody knew what had happened. Everyone was gossiping about us, but Matei didn't seem to understand that, or care. He was proud he had given me what I 'deserved', that he had punished me for my mistakes. I was so ashamed I didn't want to leave the flat. Yet I had to.

On the eve of the day our status in Denmark was to be decided in court, Matei appeared on the path coming from the camp, downcast. When he drew near, I could see he was drunk on wine and self-pity. I tried to cheer him up; I couldn't understand why he was so depressed, especially since we didn't have any illusions about the outcome.

I tried to console him. "You have your chance with Australia. It really just comes down to thinking what we can do to extend our stay here, at least for a little while." We thought of visiting Mr. Gabrielsen again, to see if he had any more tricks up his sleeve, but the day before we were to meet him we were informed that Matei had an interview at the Australian Embassy.

It would be a technical interview and while Fanel still visited Matei daily, I didn't think that you could learn a trade so fast. We were therefore very anxious. Fanel, who spoke English well, accompanied us to the embassy. We asked if he could participate in the interview as a replacement for the official interpreter, but were told that wasn't possible. All was not lost though, as we had met the woman who was the official interpreter before on various occasions and had explained our anxiety about the process. She arrived on the next train, and we just had a chance to plead with her to do her best to help Matei.

Fanel and I stayed in the waiting room while Matei and the interpreter disappeared into an office within the embassy building. He sat at the table with his head propped between his hands, while I walked round and round the room, unable to sit still under the tension. Suddenly, I felt free. Fanel lifted his head and said, "He's finished!" Ten minutes later the elevator door opened and Matei appeared, happily holding the interpreter's arm.

"How was it?" I burst out.

"Not hard. And at the end they said, 'We'll see you in Australia.'"

How much happiness can flood your soul in an instant! "When?" I asked.

"In a month, two at the most."

Although I couldn't see why, Matei went the next day to see Mr. Gabrielson. It was also my birthday, and as I had done the trip several times myself, I expected him home in the evening. But he didn't show up. I had prepared a special meal, and since I didn't want to be alone, I invited Kaiwan and Naser around.

Matei came back late the following evening and I asked him what had happened. Had there been some bad news, was he sick, where did he stay, how did he pay for the accommodation? Lately I had let him deal with our finances, but according to my calculations, he should have had about 4,000 kroners on him. He confessed that on his way back he had stopped on Odense Island and had spent the night and the money with a girl who used to be our neighbour at the camp there. I was upset about the money; he was free to do as he pleased but it wasn't fair to spend our money. My mind was now made up to separate from him, but I think that if he had tried to change a little, to win me back, I would have thought twice. On this occasion, when I saw that he was genuinely regretful, I tried to forget it.

Now we were waiting for the approval to come through from Canberra. Three months passed without any news, good or bad. During this time I kept in touch with Mişu, and nothing changed there either; in spite of all his promises, still I didn't have any certainty from him about anything. Finally, we got word from Australia, but it wasn't what we were expecting. The application had been rejected, without any explanation. In shock, I ran to the phone to call Dragos in Canada. I asked him to phone Canberra and ask for details; it was simply not possible to get such an outcome after the interview had been so successful.

We spent a terrible few days with all the old uncertainty back in our lives. Then we received a call. Dragos had tracked down the director of the immigration office, who told him to re-send the papers to Australia because the first set had been lost. There would be more waiting, more uncertainty, but there was nothing else to be done. It was now October and through the skill and grace of Mr. Gabrielson, we managed to get permission to stay in the camp until the following summer. By this time any reservations I had about getting myself and Anca to New Zealand were gone and I again called Mişu for some news. There was nothing, no good news, but he was confident his lawyer would resolve things. I could do nothing but wait and see.

Fanel and Jeni had left for Canada. I was on good terms with Gelu, but we weren't friends. Kaiwan was very supportive and understanding, however, and always ready to listen even though she had her own problems. It is very seldom that you meet true friends, and I was lucky to know Kaiwan at a time when I really needed someone like her.

During this period I had another dream. Gelu, Matei and I were behind the stores, it was night-time and while we were walking around, the police came. Scared, we scattered into the darkness. I ran with Matei, then I realised Gelu was not with us. Looking back, I saw him flanked by two policemen and then disappearing in the dark. We walked towards the camp, but there was a ditch in front of us. Matei jumped over it first, and then gave me a hand to help me jump as well. I woke up and said to myself, "We will succeed, but Gelu will be deported."

After I described my dream to Matei, he in turn told me what he had dreamt the same night: he was at home, and was hopping mad at the thought that I wanted to leave for New Zealand, when he glanced at the peg where his father's coat hung and saw it move as if somebody was inside. Then he heard his father say, "It's okay, let her go. She has stuff to do; you know that and, don't forget, you have Australia."

I took heart from this that Matei would accept our different paths. I started to sing once more, and rummage through the Romanian fairytale books to read to Anca. I went for bike rides, I had a new lease on life and there was no doubt in my mind that the visa was on its way.

One morning early I was on my bike when I met a Romanian man who had obtained permanent residency in Denmark and who now lived not far from the camp.

"Have you heard about Gelu?" he asked me. I hadn't.

"They have deported him. Back to the old country. This morning at six, the police surrounded the camp, burst into their room and accompanied them to Bucharest, to be sure they would not come back."

A few times I had tried to warn him to take precautionary measures. Just a few months back, the police had tried to deport him, but with the help of some influential people he had escaped, and I was amazed by the self-assurance he projected, relying on a few Danish friends. Now, when I heard what had happened, I thought, when you don't do anything, fate decides for you.

I spent the best part of my days with Kaiwan. Anca went to the camp kindergarten, and was very proud of the interpreter role she had achieved among the children there.

Things were the same as usual with Matei. He did not give up drinking, and he started fights with or without a reason. I needed him so much; to share with him my thoughts, my hopes and my fears, all the problems that had re-surfaced as a result of the fact that time was passing without a clear response either from Australia or New Zealand. Sometimes when I couldn't bear it any longer I would run to the phone and call Mişu, but I didn't know him well enough to unburden my soul, and besides he was so far away.

Around this time I started going to the church near the camp, and so came to know Father Anton. He would talk with refugees, ask for details of our situation, invite us to his home, encourage us and pray for us. His wife received us with pleasure, and in their home I found a warm, welcoming family who surrounded us with all their love. Whenever I visited I found Father Anton busy. I gladly offered to help and soon I was at their house almost every day.

Not far from them lived a Romanian woman who had married a Dane. We'd met Rodica when we first arrived at the camp, as she would often visit her friends there. Now, she came to play a part in one of the most terrifying episodes during our time in Denmark.

A group of immigrants from Iraq and Iran suddenly obtained the green light for their immigration. But unfortunately my friends Naser and Kaiwan were not among them. Naser had suffered greatly under Saddam's regime. He became very agitated now, fearful that they would be sent back to Iraq. No matter how calm and gentle Kaiwan was, she couldn't calm him down.

Then, around August, somebody whispered in our ears that we were targeted for deportation. What should we do? We packed everything, and searched for somewhere to hide until the visa arrived. Father Anton paid for a motel room, and we stayed indoors until dark. We stayed for a week, then another, which we paid for, and then we accepted Rodica's offer to stay in her home. We didn't know what led her to do this, since we really hardly knew her, but we were desperate and scared, and so accepted gratefully.

Mişu called and offered to send us money. I turned him down. Then, Rodica and her husband both lost their jobs. One evening at the table they said, "Elena, we're in some financial difficulty. We don't have any income. Do you think you could ask your friend in New Zealand to lend us some money? Just 20,000 kroner would be very helpful."

I didn't understand how they could ask me for something like that. But I did understand that our days there were numbered. I said I couldn't do what they wanted, that I didn't have that kind of relationship with the man in New Zealand. From then on it was clear from Rodica's behaviour that we would have to leave. One evening Matei, a little drunk, asked her why she acted that way, why she had invited us in and now wanted to send us out on the streets.

The next morning Rodica left the house very early. Immediately the thought came to me, vivid and clear, "She has gone to the camp." I told Matei my suspicions, and told him to start packing our things. The basement of the house was occupied by Jensen, a young friend of Father Anton, and since we couldn't just disappear in a flash with twenty boxes, I thought of storing them in his apartment. He wasn't in, but fortunately the door wasn't locked. I knew he would understand our need. I became increasingly agitated, thinking Matei was moving too slowly. I jumped in to help him, yelling at him to hurry up. The police could show up at any time, I was sure of it. I started to pack our suitcases and most important items, and ran up and down the stairs, piling our belongings in the middle of Jensen's room. Suddenly Kaiwan showed up, very scared.

"Elena, leave right away. Rodica came to the camp and informed the police."

We simply couldn't carry everything. Anca, made nervous by all the commotion, started to cry and told me she needed to be changed. I undressed her, but then remembered that the police could appear at any time. With her more undressed than dressed and in her bare feet, I took her by the hand, and we headed back to Father Anton's house.

I was barely coherent and couldn't stop crying, but Father Anton understood what was going on and put us all in his car. But even in the state I was in I soon realised he had no idea where to take us. I watched him mumbling to himself and praying, and all I could do was follow his example. At some point, he stopped in front of a house. The door was opened by an elderly but handsome lady who invited us in and I soon realised that we were to be put up by Father Norholm's family in Stenlille, not far from Dianalund.

Father Anton assured us we would be well treated, and he was right. We stayed with two wonderful people: Father Knud, an old man with a face so full of gentleness that I couldn't take my eyes off him. I just wanted to understand where this overabundance of goodness towards everything around him came from; and Mrs. Vibekke, whose eyes sparkled with intelligence. Two days passed with these people who embraced us as their own children, two days of leisure during which we tried to be as useful as possible.

I was on the couch, trying to fix some pants for Anca, when the silence was interrupted by the shrill ring of the phone. Of course there was nothing unusual in that, but something told me that the call was about us. Mrs. Vibekke conversed very calmly with whoever was on the other end of the phone, smiling at me the whole time, trying to ease the anxiety she saw in my eyes.

"Yes," she told me, putting the phone down. "It was the police. Rodica knew that Gelu, your neighbour from camp, stayed hidden here for a while also. She told them you couldn't be any place else. I assured them I had never seen you. They couldn't doubt the words of a priest's wife, now, could they?"

I tried to be the optimist, to believe we were safe. But this time I simply was unable to let myself be lulled by illusory assurances. How could we be sure that they wouldn't come to check, without warning? I knew what could happen in such situations in Romania, and at this moment I was thinking as a Romanian would. I called Dragos to keep him abreast of what had happened, and then packed a few things, determined to leave.

Matei tried to calm me down, but nobody could get through to me in the state I was in. I looked outside. It was raining heavily, but that didn't stop me from taking Anca by the hand and walking out of the house toward the forest. It wasn't far, and Matei followed us. In a meadow, I glimpsed an animal shelter, and we headed there. My mind was working feverishly.

"Please, Matei. Go and call the police. Ask them what they want and what we can do to obtain a respite of no more than two months, just until we get the visa for Australia."

He left, and half an hour later reappeared with a very happy look on his face.

"They weren't after us to deport us. Rodica had complained and even asked for personal protection because she thought I intended to kill her!

"I explained we had far more important problems to resolve than dealing with Rodica, and that I wasn't a criminal. He asked me where we lived, and asked for my word of honour that I wouldn't go near Rodica's house. I didn't tell them where we lived, but said they shouldn't have any doubts about Rodica since we didn't want to ever see or hear from her again."

"OK," I said. "But they were planning to deport us."

"The priest himself went to the police headquarters in Ringsted, and gave his guarantee that we are waiting for the visa. As long as they don't incur any costs with our upkeep – that is, we don't stay in the camp – as long as they are certain we are going to leave their country, they will let us be. He was very helpful and nice, the policeman."

I returned home a little calmer, but nobody could convince me to sleep inside the house. I had seen the loft above the animal barn, and I decided to sleep in the hay. I climbed the ladder and set up a comfortable sleeping arrangement for Anca and me, and we slept there for two nights. Matei slept in the house.

The next day, Father Anton let us know that he had found two secure places for us to move to. He laughed as he saw me struggling down the stairs with a couple of suitcases.

"Come on, if you can sleep a couple of nights in the barn, these two suitcases should be nothing to you." I was asking myself, where was Matei? Why wasn't he helping me? Why was everything that he should have been doing left for me to do, and he didn't even appreciate it? Everything I did, he took for granted, as if that was simply the way things happened.

Anca and I went in a car with the priest's wife, and Matei with Father Anton. At an intersection, we separated; we were to go to Copenhagen and Matei was to be put up in Kalundborg.

A strikingly beautiful lady opened the door to our new temporary lodging. Dr Anette Marsden had a delicate, classical beauty with a wide, open smile and a matching nature. She showed us a room on the upper level of her house, where we also had a sink, and the bathroom across the hallway. The next morning around the breakfast table we met her entire family. She had two children, a boy and a girl who very soon became Anca's friends. After breakfast we went to church with the whole family, and we did so every Sunday during the time we stayed in their house. On workday mornings they would go down to the basement, where Anette's and her husband's medical office was.

I tried to be of some use in the house. It was late autumn, and the last of the leaves and fruit covered the entire back lawn. I gathered the fruit and did what I could around the house, which was far from enough for these wonderful people who had so trustingly given us shelter.

One day on our return home from church we took a detour, and stopped to pick up a little boy – aged around eight or nine – who was accompanied by a young girl. I understood he was their son. He lived at a special boarding school from where they brought him home for weekends and holidays. He wasn't violent; he lived in a world of his own, set apart from everything around him. Deep in my soul I shared his mother's pain, and I understood that she had placed all her hopes in God.

Matei was staying with a missionary and his mother, and although like us he was treated as a member of the family, he was lonely. He called me every night, and both of us shared the fear that Rodica, in her hatred, could still cause us harm. The slightest hint dropped at the Australian Embassy regarding my intention to go to New Zealand could have wrecked our plans.

Other than this worry, those were days of relative peace and quiet. They gave me the space to think about my intention that once in Australia we would part company. Does that really have to happen? I would ask myself. One weekend, when my hosts were expecting guests, I took Anca to see Matei. But I was still afraid. I had been hurt, and I didn't think that Matei would change. He had shown me his darker side, and it frightened me. On the other hand, my talks with Mişu were comforting. When he said, "I understand, I know what you want, I would do anything to get your children by your side," the hope of being able to right the wrong I had done drove me in that direction.

Finally, we were notified about the medical check-up that all emigrants went through. At last, after so long, could it finally be happening? I welcomed the news with relief rather than enthusiasm, since it had been so long coming, and I was by now exhausted. We had a month's notice of the appointment, and during this time we had to change our hosts. One evening at the end of October, accompanied by Father Anton, we arrived at a house in Dianalund, on the other side of the forest from the camp we had fled not long before.

Father Anton introduced us to two middle-aged ladies, Lene and Brigitte, whom we found cutting up fruit to be dried.

"This is Elena, who doesn't speak Danish but understands it, and this is Anca, who is like a real Dane."

It was an extremely peaceful atmosphere. Everything about the house seemed to say, "You're home. Can you believe it?" I felt like I was recuperating after a grave illness, and everything, material or human, seemed to contribute to my complete recovery.

With Lene and Brigitte I saw how you can live well, how you can be happy with modest means. When she wasn't working, Brigitte spent a lot of time with Anca; she told her stories, taught her to crochet, and, importantly, she would discipline her. Very often, the smell of warm bread and home baking filled the house, but Anca never got anything unless it was at the table, for lunch or dinner.

As always, I tried to make myself as useful as possible, and I started by splitting firewood and stacking it in the shed for the winter. I gathered late apples and cut them up for drying and set up the vegetable garden for the new season.

The cold season started, and the first snowflakes lost no time making their appearance. I took full advantage of the pleasant warmth from the hearth, which I didn't let cool down.

Matei wrote and called, insisting I should not go to New Zealand. I understood he was lonely, and that we, Anca and I, were his life. Without us he was vulnerable and it was hard for him to find his inner equilibrium. But I asked myself what would happen when he forgot these things, because I knew that once we were together, he would soon forget how much he had missed us.

Since we were so close to the camp, Kaiwan crossed the forest daily to visit us. She had gained legal residency in Denmark, and in a few weeks was to move to a new place. We were both more at peace, in secure circumstances, and were making plans for the future. For her it seemed everything was clear. For me, the future lay hidden. I was at the start of a path I didn't know, nor did I know what was waiting at the end.

On the eve of our departure from Denmark, for my birthday, Brigitte and Lene organised a special farewell meal. Dr. Marsden's family visited and it was wonderful to be able to celebrate with these kind people, who had appeared in our lives at such a difficult time, and offered us a helping hand.

Before leaving, I had a discussion with Remus about Mişu. I wasn't feeling so sure about him and his promises so I felt Remus should wait before taking the decision to leave Romania. Remus said Mişu had called him, assuring him that he would be supporting us, and that he would also pay for their fare from Canada to New Zealand.

"How could I not help you?" Remus told me what Mişu had said. "You are fellow countrymen, what else can I do? Don't think of money. You can pay me back from your first salary. This isn't going to break me."

Remus said everything was ready for him and Lili to travel to Canada, to stay with Dragos, from where he could come to New Zealand.

I told him he should wait until he heard from me once I got there.

"It's too late," he said. "Besides, Lili is adamant we do this." I wasn't happy, but I didn't say any more, knowing it wouldn't make a difference.

The Danish police paid for half of our plane fare, and two young police officers accompanied us to the steps of the plane. We had many, many pieces of luggage, and it was actually a great help having them there to get them all loaded. They were both pleasant men and kind, and confirmed to me yet again, the good impression I had of the Danish people. The place had grown on me, and remains as a memory engraved on my soul.

17

Melbourne, Australia! I simply could not understand how it could be so hot. The light was blinding, there were flowers everywhere, and raucous birds. When I saw in someone's yard a flock of parrots surrounding a cage like those we used to keep pigeons in at home, it just confirmed how surreal everything was. Just a few days before, I had been riding through a white forest, my hands freezing on the bike handlebars; now I was walking in a city blazing with colour, in full summer.

Mihaela and Mihai hadn't changed. They welcomed us and were ready to help in whatever way they could. Mihaela accompanied us to make sure we could get the paperwork done for the support we were entitled to, and for my and Anca's departure.

I had decided to leave in a week. Mișu was calling daily, and told me that I had obtained New Zealand residency.

My departure was certain, but still I suffered doubts about leaving Matei. How did it come to this? Where had we gone wrong? We had fought and overcome so much to be together, and now we were parting. What was the point of going through all we had gone through if we weren't staying together? Where did the love go, that had given us the courage and strength to face a lifetime of challenges? I knew he loved me, but I also knew that our life together would have been full of fighting and uncertainty. I had been hurt, gravely hurt, by the man for whom I had left everything – family, security, country – everything, behind. In the end, I knew I would have had to leave him.

Although I had gotten over most of what had happened, it seemed now that my memories were coming back with even greater intensity. Yet while this firmed up my resolve, whenever I saw him sad and upset, I suffered. If he had said, "Please stay, I'll do anything to make it work, I realise I have to change," or something, anything, in that vein to really make me think, maybe I would have relented. And then everything might have been different. Who knows? I thought about this more than once, after discovering the surprise which awaited me in New Zealand.

I stepped on the bus to Sydney at six o'clock on a summer evening, December 1993. Anca was with me, and Matei had come to see us off. I couldn't look either of them in the face. Why was I separating them? What was calling me to this unknown country at the end of the world? I didn't know anyone there, just a man who had given me hope, in whom I'd seen my only chance of having my sons with me and so to right the wrong I had done. Although I was lifted by Mişu's many promises, some questions also came up. "Ohhh, I've taken some steps, just in case you try to trick me," he said once in response to a question I must have asked about how he was prepared to do so much. I didn't understand his response, but didn't dwell on it. I would soon learn what a mistake that was.

"In forty years, I've never put a nail in the house," he said once. "It's a little messy, but I'll buy a bottle of wine for you to drink on the way home." I assumed he was joking. He was an old and lonely man. Things probably wouldn't be very clean. But I didn't mind pitching in.

On another occasion he said, "It was me that sold out the Greeks who came by ship."

"What on earth is he talking about?" I asked myself.

Looking back, there were many, many other instances that should have been enough to stop me. But I was blinded by my desire to do something to have all my children beside me, and felt acutely the lack of any real moral support as I tried to find a path to a future that included all of us.

But now I felt I had no choice.

The trip passed fairly easily. We stopped a few times for half an hour, and I watched a movie while Anca slept. But the usual thoughts stole upon me. "Where am I going, who are these people?" I also thought painfully of Matei; I didn't have the right to take his child away from him, but I couldn't let her hear and see what happened between us either. I knew his suffering was immense, but still it was a choice that had to be made.

At six thirty in the morning we stepped down at Wollongong, where we were met by Mişu's friends. I tried to start a conversation with the man, but he didn't seem in the mood and so I got wrapped up in my thoughts. Suddenly, I heard him say, "Madam, do you know Mişu?"

"Not personally," I answered, "but in the past two years we've been talking on the phone every couple of days."

He didn't say anything more.

His wife greeted us merrily, and without hiding her curiosity studied me from head to toe.

"When Mişu sees you, he'll fall down, he'll die!" she told me in a sweet Moldovan accent.

I couldn't help feeling these people were scared. But what of? What kind of person is this Mişu? I stayed in their house for six days and as I got to know them better, I again asked myself what kind of man Mişu could be, with such friends. They both stayed up late, drinking. They had asked Mişu for money "for your upkeep" during the six days. My understanding was that they were deeply indebted to him from the time when they had lived in New Zealand. I felt them looking at me as if I was some kind of strange animal. Of course I didn't understand why. In the evening I would go to bed early, and I knew that around the table, which was in the next room, they were discussing me. I kept asking them whether they could tell me something about Mişu. "Oh, he's very, very kind," they would say. But I felt that something was being kept from me.

We stayed there for so long because Mişu insisted I couldn't leave yet. But I didn't understand why. I had an Australian visa and could enter New Zealand at any time, but it took nearly a week for Mişu to understand this fact. It was only when we finally left, and were sitting in the plane, that it really hit me that I wasn't going to see Matei again. During my six days in Wollongong, we had frequently talked on the phone. Only the fact that I had promised Remus I was going to be in New Zealand gave me the strength to go on; otherwise I think I would have turned back. Remus was already in Canada waiting for me to sort things out so he and Lili could come to New Zealand. All I wanted now was to get there as soon as possible and see what fate had in store for me.

Nobody was waiting for us at Wellington airport. I headed to an information booth, where, using sign language because I didn't speak English, and didn't have money, I eventually gained permission to use their phone. I called Mişu.

"I'm coming right away," he said.

He'd bought the tickets, so he knew what time we would arrive. And yet he wasn't here? I was unhappy, but I didn't want to think anything bad. I decided to wait calmly. Half an hour later, I saw an old man come through the door. He looked as if he had just escaped from a brawl. His open coat flapped around him, and a winter hat sat on his head even though it was summer, looking as though it was ready to fall off at any second. His hands, which seemed unusually long, reached out as if looking for something. I didn't expect Prince Charming, but what I saw was grotesque! As he came nearer, I saw how dirty his hands and clothes were. But he had a smile on his face.

It was getting dark as we got to his car. I remembered another remark from our phone conversations: "When you arrive, I won't take you straight home. Until it gets dark I will show you the city."

It was close to Christmas, and the whole city seemed to be getting ready for the biggest holiday of the year. As we drove, I looked at Mişu from the corner of my eye, asking myself how he could have such dirty fingernails. His large, knotty hands were in continuous motion, reminding me of a puppet. I don't usually comment on people's appearances, but everything about Mişu seemed to be unnatural. Something was not right.

I turned back to Anca, sitting in the rear, and saw a puzzled little face that seemed to ask me, "What are we doing here, far from all who loved me and whom I loved back?"

He stopped in front of a house and honked the horn, and a small elderly woman opened the door.

She introduced herself as Dana, and showed us in.

It was a modestly furnished and very well-maintained house. In an armchair in a corner sat Vica, a good-looking old man with a gentle way of speaking. Both of them, Dana and Vica, studied me carefully.

"Tell me something about Mişu's house. Is it as welcoming?" I asked Dana.

"Well, you will see. It's a house." They looked at each other.

It was long after dark when we left to go home. We came to a narrow road, in what I would later learn was Wellington's Te Aro Valley, filled with houses crowded right up next to each other in the darkness. The car stopped in front of a house that, even in the dim light from neighbouring houses, I could see was old and derelict, patched with corrugated roofing iron, the paint peeling and with gaps in the wooden boards like broken teeth. A set of steps climbed up to the door, which was set well back in the darkness. It depressed me before I was even out of the car.

Mişu opened the door, and I was struck by the strong, sharp smell and the sudden din of barking dogs that greeted the sound of our arrival. At a roar from Mişu, the noise fell silent. Seven Pomeranians started fawning at his legs and then came closer to Anca and me, measuring us up with fearful looks. I looked around to see where we were. It was little better than a shed, and a dirty one at that.

"When you get here, I will have a bottle of cognac ready for you so that you don't see very well." I remembered Mişu saying that once during our phone calls.

The hallway was dark, but I could see strips of torn wallpaper, and mess and dirt everywhere. The floor was covered neither by a rug nor linoleum; what was left was a mixture of what had once been both. From the hallway, two doors opened to the sides and one at the end. The two led to "bedrooms" and the third to a room that normally would have been the dining room. To get in, you had to jump over a cardboard box that was placed as a barrier to the dogs. From the supposed dining room, a door opened to a hall where you could hardly move for the piles of bottles and stuffed-full plastic bags stacked to the ceiling. Another door led to the dogs' room and the third to the "kitchen", "bathroom" and another room behind a door I couldn't open, because it was blocked with more boxes that were randomly thrown on top of each other.

I couldn't see the state of everything, but what I could see was enough to make me dizzy. I couldn't believe it. I opened the bathroom door, and stood stock still on the threshold. I had lived in the country, where people were extremely busy and lived and worked in some pretty rough conditions; I had seen a lot more in my travels across Europe, from eastern Romania to Calais, from France to Denmark, but this was something new and unexpected. Saying every surface was dark and slimy is nothing compared to how the bath tub, toilet and sink looked. You could hardly guess they were there, under the layers of dirt. The walls were so grimy that you couldn't know what colour they had been originally, and there were spiders everywhere that had clearly felt at home for years. Compared to what I saw now, the house of Matei's old, invalid parents when I first arrived was like a spotless, orderly palace.

"In forty years, I haven't done anything." Another of Mişu's admissions by phone, that I simply couldn't take literally, now stared me in the face. I wondered what I would see the next day, and shivered at the thought.

I tried to switch off my horror. I knew I had no choice, nowhere else to go. I also didn't want to start thinking about what I had gotten myself into, in believing in this revolting old man. I took a large towel from my suitcase, wrapped myself in it, and started to clean the bathroom. In the dining room, on the darkened, greasy table, next to where some piles of papers had been pushed aside, I found Mişu had put out some canned food and imitation black caviar. "I feed my dogs caviar," rang in my head. Is that what we were now?

I wanted to give Anca a glass of milk, and since I couldn't find anything clean, picked up some of the plates, glasses and cutlery that seemed to have gone unwashed for years and cleaned them, ready for the next morning. Then I asked where we could rest. Mişu led us out proudly, wanting to show me the house.

"This is my bedroom, which you can use, and Anca can sleep next door on the couch."

"Why?" I asked. I don't know how I looked or what my tone of voice was, but I stayed in that room with Anca. How to begin to describe it? It was a room with a bed in the middle, nothing unusual in that, and there were a few other pieces of furniture, but with the exception of the wardrobe, the rest couldn't be seen for the papers, boxes and rags that were thrown in heaps on top of them. Books, old folders chewed by mice, worn out shoes, others so dusty that you could hardly distinguish their colour, all were piled up on something that I suspected were cupboards, or on the floor, leaving only a narrow walkway around the bed.

I saw a few torn pieces of something that had once been a rug, the curtains hung in tatters as if somebody had pulled at them purposelessly, while the walls were almost bare, leaving the wooden skeleton of the house exposed. The bed was filled with dog hair, but fortunately I had some bed sheets in my suitcases.

I was sad and frightened, and Anca looked at me as if asking, "Is this the house you told me about? Are we really going to stay here?"

That night, I could hardly close my eyes. I had to gather my thoughts and cool down. Of course I'd expected things to be tough as a new immigrant, re-adapting to a normal life in a new country where I didn't yet speak the language. And I was ready to face these challenges head on. But nothing I'd experienced had prepared me for what I'd landed in. Eventually I must have dozed off, because in my dream a figure appeared and handed me a box, small and wooden, like a jewellery box, but dusty. I couldn't quite make out the person's face who now urged me to open it.

"No, I don't want to," I said.

"Open it, and you'll find something valuable," the person said.

"It could be anything. I don't want to touch it, I don't want anything."

I woke to an uproar: loud music, the dogs barking furiously and Mişu yelling at the top of his voice, trying to make them stop. Daylight streamed through the window and the holes in the curtains. I got up, realising that what I had seen the night before hadn't been a bad dream. I peeked inside the wardrobe doors and saw all the clothes inside were covered by a thick layer of dust. Most showed signs of being moth-eaten. I changed and prepared to set off on a reconnaissance mission. Anca woke as well, but I asked her to stay put until I had done some cleaning, and so I could prepare something for her to eat.

I started with the room where Mişu had slept. There was a shabby, broken couch, two former armchairs – now resting places for boxes full of bottles which themselves were covered with old junk. Above the fireplace, under the heavy dust, I glimpsed a beautiful woodcarving of Romania's coat of arms. If he was such a royalist, I asked myself, why had he worked for those who had deposed the king, for the first communist regime? I knew the story from Jean, and over the long phone calls, Mişu had gradually confirmed it: he had been an agent of the first communist regime in the country, he had worked in Germany and at some point, although I didn't find out why, he decided to emigrate to New Zealand. Mişu said the fireplace was home to a possum that visited him from time to time. Most of the rest was rubbish that had accumulated over the years.

I moved on to the dining room. Opening a refrigerator, the stink from dirty trays of dog food and two large pots with boiled bones hit me. There was a second refrigerator intended for humans, but it was just as dirty, the dishes inside just as slimy, and there were two other pots with smelly dog food. I shuddered at the thought of how long it would take me to clean the place up so that everything looked even half decent.

Between the two refrigerators, there was a full freezer.

"I have been stocking up for a couple of years, maybe longer," Mişu's telephone voice had told me.

On top of the fridges and freezer were mountains of plastic bags, reaching up to the ceiling. The table I had seen the night before was only partially usable, just a little corner. The rest was covered by more piles of newspapers, paper, canned food, a radio set that you could hardly see for all the papers around it, bottles, jars and many bags of bread. On the opposite wall was a built-in cupboard, above which a few pieces of mice-chewed salami hung from the ceiling.

"It's better if it's drier," Mişu said, following my eyes.

The holes in the lino revealed rotting floorboards, so I stepped carefully, thinking my feet could sink through at any time. I looked into the dogs' room: there was a bed made of planks, a broken mattress, a dresser and on the ground, many torn, dirty rags, thick with dog hair.

I turned to the kitchen, a narrow little galley. As I tried to get to the sink, I felt my foot going into a hole.

"Be careful! There was a plank there, but you moved it last night," Mişu told me.

"Why don't you put up a sign to warn people who come into the kitchen?" I asked angrily.

"Because nobody comes here."

The water pipes ran alongside the walls and were black with grease and smoke. Under the sink, among spider webs and a thick layer of dirt, I found a mixture of mugs and glasses, all yellow with years of grease. I pushed open the door of the small room by the kitchen that was blocked with boxes. I discovered torn mattresses, broken mirrors, an old cabinet with a missing door, piles of empty glasses.

On the phone once he had told me that for some reason a search of his home had been made. When the two men left, one of them had asked him, "Hey, man, don't you ever throw away anything?" I could hardly have imagined they were referring to what I could see now.

Back at the sink I wondered where to start. Anca had to eat.

"Well? What do you think? Do you like it?" Mişu said behind me. "And why did you dress so well? I have some leftover clothes from former tenants, you can use them."

I wasn't especially well dressed. I simply had clean clothes on.

Again I looked around and concluded that trying to clean up would mean working for months, not a day or two. Anca was now outside in the sun playing with the dogs. I asked Mişu to go with her and buy her something to eat. In the meantime, I started to sort through the various piles that were lying around everywhere; anything good I kept so that it could be cleaned; the rest went into three bags that I filled in less than an hour. The fridges were emptied; nothing was fresh or fit to be eaten.

When he came back and saw what I'd done, Mişu was horrified. "What are you doing? Put it all back!" His face was a picture of disbelief. "Everything is expensive. It has to be eaten." He gave me a chicken that he'd fished out of the bag. I looked at the label and saw it had been bought two years previously.

"I'm not eating that," I said.

"Why not?" Again, he was visibly shocked.

"Because it's too old."

"What? The American army freezes stuff for two years. Why shouldn't we?"

What was I to do? I knew that Remus was in Canada, waiting to hear how things were going and when they would be able to join us. After the promises Mişu had made him, it would be very hard for him to understand the true state of the situation we were in. They couldn't stay in Canada, and their plane ticket to wherever they would go next had to be paid for. Mişu had thought of everything in detail to lure us in. I had also totally fallen for his offer of "selfless" help and his desire to escape loneliness. In the predicament I had been in, it was wasn't too hard to believe in someone else suffering, and wanting to do something about it. Then there was the fact that over the two years we'd been talking on the phone he'd spent thousands of dollars. I'd been desperate to escape the state of uncertainty we were living in, but, more than anything else, I wanted my children beside me.

I felt guilty towards them. I had hurt them. I had hurt what I loved most in the world, and all the time I had desperately tried the impossible; to rebuild a puzzle that was missing some of its pieces. My children didn't ask for anything, but I wanted to do so much for them, to put right the mistakes I'd made in letting myself be driven by my instincts. I never stopped to think that there might be mistakes in life that cannot be fixed. I had to try.

I had set things in motion with Mişu and I could not back out. Instead I tried to make sense of where I was. If I could make this work and bring Remus here, I thought, then perhaps the rest of it would work out as well.

"Why are you living this way?" I asked Mişu. "How can you possibly put up with these conditions?" I asked him.

"What conditions?"

I couldn't believe he didn't see a problem.

"The immigration people came. They were quite content. It's not snowing, not raining indoors. What more do you want?"

18

I PHONED CANADA, TRYING TO EXPLAIN HOW THINGS WERE here, but I didn't understand how hard it was to imagine these conditions if you couldn't see them. I cried and screamed but nobody would believe that in the twentieth century, in a civilized country, somebody with Mişu's pretensions could live in such filth.

I didn't have to stay there. But there was nowhere else I could go. I didn't know anyone. I didn't have any money. I didn't speak the language. I had no idea what, if any, options there were in this country. I was stuck.

"Do what you think is best for you, Mum," was the response. "If you want to return to Australia, you do that. We'll manage."

That just infuriated me. "They don't believe me," I told myself. "They think I'm making it up because I want to go to back to Australia, to Matei." Looking back, I can see now they were saying the right thing. But at the time, it just made me angry. Possibly my reaction was a consequence of the betrayal I felt from Mişu. I no longer trusted anyone. So instead of taking my children's advice, I decided I would stay, and we would all see what would happen.

The shock was so powerful that as long as I was close to Mişu, and for years after, I felt the effects of a deep change in me. I was tormented by thoughts that nothing I said or did was right, that people judged my every gesture, every action. I lived with the fear that something unknown was lurking around the corner, about to come at me, but I had no idea what it was. I don't know if I can say I've fully recovered from that feeling. In my confused state I felt I couldn't run, so all I could do was be ready to fight. I lived in a permanent state of nervous tension, and didn't think I would ever again experience a sense of personal calmness and peace. I didn't accept anything anyone told me, especially Mişu. He saw how indecisive I became, and started to repeat a refrain he was sure I would enjoy. "I'll fix the houses, and then I'll sell one. You bring your boy here, and maybe the other one as well." I don't know if he knew how false it sounded, or if he was singing a tune to deliberately torment me.

"I don't want to see you," I said. "And don't promise me anything else. Just try to honour everything you said you would do. Pay Remus's fare from Canada, since you with your countless letters and phone calls convinced them to go there. And don't forget the private school for Anca. How could you promise so much and do nothing? What kind of person are you? 'Everything for the children's future'," I would finish, bitterly quoting his slogan that seemed now to have been lifted from some communist propaganda document.

"I have the money," he said. "I'll do everything you want – but we must have an official marriage. It cannot be done otherwise. They won't be able to come from Canada."

"You must be mad. I'm not going to marry you."

"I have arranged everything for December the nineteenth," he went on, undaunted.

Matei called, desperately trying to dissuade me from doing anything. But now I heard everything as if through a haze. And why should I believe Matei? He'd lied to me as well. I felt trapped, with no way of making decisions of my own, for my own good.

Along with Dana, one of the only people I felt I could talk to at this time was Desiree, the wife of one of Mişu's sons, Stefan. He was the only one who still kept in touch with their father. The others, according to Dana, didn't want anything to do with him. For fourteen years, Mişu had dragged his wife through various courts to try and prove she wasn't competent to raise their children. He wanted custody of them, but didn't accomplish anything other than finding out they were not his, and mentally tormenting them. No one who didn't know Mişu well could understand why he had done that. But to me it was clear. He wanted to prove he was right, and he especially wanted to revenge himself on his wife for deserting him.

Desiree was young and blonde, with ivory skin. She had a warm smile and, as I was to find out, a warm soul to go with it. From when we first met she tried to support and encourage me. She had four children, much to Anca's delight, and as Anca would be starting school in a month, being among other children could only help her. Moreover, this way she wasn't around to witness the fights between Mişu and me, fights that took place every hour of the day.

I went into town with Desiree so she could show me the shops. Everything seemed surreal, floating by as if in some brightly lit dream. I heard her ask Mişu for something, and understood she was insisting that he buy a Christmas tree and a gift for Anca. I just couldn't get involved. Desiree picked out a teddy bear for Anca and helped to decorate the tree while I was like a robot. I ate,

I walked, I talked. But I didn't think. On Christmas Eve I was in bed with Anca. I sat in the middle of the bed making great efforts to smile and talk with her. Stefan came in to wish us Merry Christmas. I looked at him dumbfounded, not reacting in any way. Christmas? What was he talking about? Christmas was an occasion for joy. Here everything was sad, dirty and old.

Dana called to invite us for Christmas dinner. I was glad to get away, thinking that for a few hours at least, I would be able to exist in a quiet, pleasant atmosphere.

I could tell they pitied me. I learned from Dana that she had wanted to call me in Denmark, to describe Mişu and his way of life.

She told me about someone they knew who had gone to see Mişu for some reason or other, and who after leaving had come round to Dana's house, shouting as soon as she got in the door, "My God, I heard Mişu wants to bring somebody over from Denmark! Please tell that person, beg her not to come. I can't believe what I've just seen in that man's house."

"But I think you wouldn't have understood," she said. "And you might have blamed us for interfering."

Thinking about how my children were having trouble understanding from their own mother how bad things were, and how desperate I was to find some kind of future for ourselves, I am sure she was right.

Dana went on. "Judging by your letters, which he read to everyone, I knew you were not for him. I told him that. But you can see what kind of man he is. You can't talk to him." Her eyes tried to hold mine. "I am sorry," she said.

I felt humiliated by what I heard, degraded. He had practically dictated the letters I'd written him, suggesting the content and telling me "the lawyer wants them like that, they need to sound more convincing, affectionate – if you want to get a visa." And then he used them to demonstrate to the people he knew how much I "loved" him. How naïve I had been. It was hard knowing that these same people knew the true extent of how I had been tricked.

Dana could certainly see how unhappy I was. She invited us around almost every evening; I found her and Vica very good listeners, and I would tell them stories about home. That would help me forget I was at the end of the world, that my soul was aching, that my predicament was so confused, that I didn't have the strength to do anything about it even if I knew what I had to do.

Mişu and Vica would doze off in their armchairs while I told Dana fragments of my life at home, especially when Matei and I had been living together. I always felt Mişu was listening to every word though. That didn't bother me, as there was nothing wrong in what I said. I never thought that somebody would use such recollections, which were as beautiful as they were innocent, to discredit me with others. But that is exactly what Mişu did, of course. He would stop and tell others stories about me, using details from my past to misrepresent the truth to suit his purpose.

After Christmas, Mişu told me I should meet the lawyer who had helped him obtain my New Zealand residency, and who would explain to me why we had to get married.

I had not met this man, Mr. R, yet, so I had nothing against it. He seemed very genuine, but I didn't understand anything from the conversation he and Mişu had in front of me. When Mişu told me, "Look, he says you cannot bring Remus over if we don't go ahead with the marriage, even if it's only one of convenience," I believed him. In spite of what I now knew of Mişu, I never thought for a moment he would translate something different from what he had been told.

On January 11 we were at the registrar's office. In a daze, I remember being asked by a lady to repeat something that she read. Mr. R, who had agreed to be a witness, offered me a bouquet of flowers. Afterwards, we went to Desiree's house. There we found Dana with Vica and some other people who Mişu introduced to me as his friends. I retreated to another room, trying to understand what there was left for me to do. But I couldn't gather my thoughts. I felt completely helpless, without any will of my own. Large tears fell down my cheeks. I heard Mişu tell everyone that it was because of Matei that I had been resisting him, and then say the most incredible things about a man he had never met. He complained that I talked with Matei on the phone, and showed them the cheque which that morning, before going to the registrar's office, he had written for the plane tickets for Remus and his wife. This was news to me – I had forgotten that their trip had to be paid for. So I'd gotten married in exchange for the $2,000.

Mişu was exultant. He had succeeded. He sang and danced and wasn't bothered that I "played angry" as he described it to others, in explaining my absence. The first thought that surfaced in my daze was how I could make him suffer.

Around eleven at night we left to go home, and so the ordeal began.

"We are married, we have to sleep in the same bed," he would shout, puffing himself up. He was taking his role very seriously, seeing himself as my husband. At first I tried to tell him calmly, "Mişu, the part doesn't suit you. You tried to portray yourself as decent and selfless to make me believe in you, but—

"What? I paid—"

"Never. You lied to me, you promised me...." I was so angry now I simply lost the words. I could only keep repeating, "Never. Never. Never."

I preferred to go to bed early and read before falling asleep.

Mişu would only go to bed after midnight. I would be fast asleep when he would touch the quilt, waking me up. He would make some kind of hand gesture, meaning he was waiting for me in his bedroom next door. I would cover my head without saying anything, and in a few minutes, he would appear again, insisting, clamouring. I would remind him about our understanding, and then the shouts would start, "I paid the plane fare. I'm going to do everything for you. You have to—"

"I don't want anything. I don't want anything from you. Leave me alone."

Awakened by the noise, Anca would start to cry. I would throw anything I could find at him, and finally he would go and read the newspaper in the dining room. He would turn the radio up, the dogs would bark, and there was nothing I could do to get away from the din and anger other than take Anca out into the street. Fortunately it was summer, and we could walk up and down the street without worrying too much about the cold.

"What sin brought me here?" I would ask myself as we walked, waiting for Mişu to tire himself out.

On one of these night walks I thought I could try to clean up Mişu's second house, next door to ours. Perhaps then Anca and I could live there. It was in a worse state, if that was possible, than Mişu's house had been. The bathroom and kitchen were covered in grime and mould, and one of the two bedrooms was unusable. Over the years the house had been inhabited by several of Mişu's friends, some of whom had left bits and pieces of their furniture behind. Most of this was crammed into a room whose walls were crumbling under the attention of the rat infestation.

I started rising very early in the mornings, to sneak next door and begin cleaning the place out to try to make it inhabitable. But one morning Mişu discovered me. I think the whole neighbourhood could hear him shouting.

"This is my fortune! Don't touch it. I've been collecting this for years and years and now you come to throw it out?"

"Is this the wealth you accumulated in fifty years? If you only were Hagi Tudose[1]. But this is all just rubbish."

With Desiree's help, I persuaded him to let me clean up the rest of the house. She helped me paint the walls, she sewed the curtains, we chose a few of the least disgusting pieces of furniture, and together we replaced the carpets. I started to cook there, and finally arranged a bedroom for Anca and me.

Towards the end of January, Anca had to start school. I had no idea about the educational system in New Zealand, nor whether the schools nearby were any good.

"Private school is out of the question," Mişu screamed. "It's far too expensive."

I never understood why he couldn't talk in a normal tone of voice. I had expected that response, after reminding him of his promise regarding this. Then he started raving on in a way that clearly showed he didn't know what needed to be done to get Anca into school.

But I didn't know either. I was getting more and more worried about what to do when one day Desiree showed up for coffee with a friend of hers who was a teacher. She said her school was a very good one, it was only five minutes' drive away, and she offered then and there to take Anca in her class.

On the morning of the first school day we presented ourselves at the principal's office, as we had been told to. As soon as he entered, Mişu started to pull out shabby photos from his equally shabby pockets to show everyone, of his family and children in Romania. I had no idea where these had come from, or what he thought he was doing. No one was interested or had time for this, nor could they understand why he was showing them these old pictures. Seeing the puzzled looks of those around us, I felt overwhelmed with shame. Finally, the principal understood why we had come, and, taking Anca by the hand, he headed for the group of kids in the class where she was to be enrolled.

On our way home, I asked Mişu why he had insisted on raising his children himself.

"Their mother didn't want them and the world had to find out."

I didn't understand.

"Yes, she left with the man she had had the kids with, without taking any of them with her. She came back in a few months, but I didn't want to give them back to her. We were in court for fourteen years."

"Why aren't you in touch with them?" I asked.

"I don't know why they don't contact me. Only the one in Christchurch, the one I lent twenty thousand dollars to, he comes, but very seldom."

Desiree later explained that none of the children wanted anything to do with him for all the years he had dragged them through the courts to satisfy his own vain ambition.

While it was a relief to have Anca at school, it also created another bone of contention. We could never, ever, get there on time. It was too far to walk, but not far to drive, and so another situation came about in which I depended upon Mişu. Every morning we would argue as I tried to get him to hurry up, and every time I heard a variation of the same reply. "I was never on time for work, and I was fine. It was fine for forty years. I always found an excuse and I managed perfectly well."

And so I would start every day angry.

After dropping Anca off at school, Mişu almost always went on into town. At first I would accompany him, but it was not long before this too became intolerable. Food was the only thing of interest to him; he bought it with pleasure, but only the things and only at the places he was accustomed to. I began to notice other stores, not just the vegetable kiosks or the food stores he knew. But we never went into them.

Once inside, his behaviour was predictable as well. He would make a beeline for the reject bin where blemished fruits and vegetables were thrown, dig his hands in and scrabble about trying to find something slightly better than garbage. If luck didn't smile on him, he would grab a few leaves for the ducks. I looked at him, and thought about either how I could get out of this situation, or how I could be more patient until I did manage to escape. He talked endlessly with anybody he met, he talked in the car so much that I couldn't even open my mouth, and anyway I didn't want to comment on all his idle talk because that would just lead to an argument.

I fought openly with him now, which was totally the wrong tactic. Useless discussions, gossip and unfounded opinion fed his soul. He was a master of these things, as well as others, much more nefarious, which I was still to find out about. His favourite subject was Matei. He would curse uncontrollably and make all kinds of accusations against Matei. Once he started, he couldn't stop. It got to the point that no matter where we were I would simply leave. Even if we were driving, I would simply open the car door and get out. I couldn't bear hearing him talking incessantly. I had had enough of useless talk with Matei, who also had a great talent for drawing me into endless, meaningless conversations that could only be stopped by physically walking away. Mişu, however, would follow me in his car, and through the open window he would start to yell, "I won't say anything else, I promise. Come back."

Usually I would return home on foot. In the evening I would write to Matei. In my current state I forgot or overlooked everything he had done to me, because I needed somebody to describe all my misfortune to. As I wrote, Mişu would slowly open the door to spy on me, but I didn't make it a secret that I was writing to Australia.

I didn't have any money, and as those letters had to be posted I would gather every cent I could find around the house, once even taking some change from the pocket of one of Mişu's coats. I finally appealed to Desiree for help. She immediately insisted Mişu give me some pocket money. For two weeks he gave me five dollars a week, "because you already have food, that's enough."

I felt I had no respite. I was tired because Mişu continued to stay up until after midnight, then the dogs would begin barking to go out early in the morning. I would let them out, but since Mişu wouldn't get up, the noise didn't stop. I was irritable and upset all the time. Around this time, after Anca had started school, I found a path leading into town that I would follow, then find a bench to rest on. I would write or simply look at the passers-by. The path passed a church, the doors of which stood wide open as if inviting me to come in. When I finally did, I found a haven of calm where I could rest from the awful situation that was weighing on me. With my soul in turmoil, I knelt, and my tears flowed without restraint. I felt God's presence there, and spoke directly to Him. "God, I know I was wrong, but please, don't leave me. I am alone, I can't make any decisions, so please decide for me."

When I left, I felt I had someone beside me, somebody inspiring me with hope and making me feel I was no longer alone in my unhappiness. I had needed to do that so much, to put down that burden and share my sorrow, even if only for a short time.

On another day I was sitting on a bench when I heard some strains of Romanian music on the air. My heart leapt at the sound, and I got up to find out where it was coming from. I soon found a man playing the panpipes. It was such an astonishing experience I burst into tears. I asked the man how he came to be there with this instrument, which is so well known in our country.

"Mr. Zamfir gave it to me, and taught me how me to play it," was all he said. I sat and listened as he played, unable to move for a long time.

Every day Mişu went to the local petrol station to collect newspapers that hadn't sold in the past day or two. The back seat of his car was always unusable, being filled with piles of these papers, some of which he gave to our neighbours and some he stored in the house.

One morning we stopped at the mechanic's workshop where Mişu knew someone. I stayed in the car, and as I had a letter for Matei stuck in a book I took it out to write the address on the envelope.

Suddenly, Mişu appeared and swooped in to snatch the envelope out of my hand.

"What are you doing?" I asked, grabbing hold of it.

He knew I was writing to Matei, I'd never made a secret of it, so once again, I could not understand his behaviour. I was furious in my surprise and frustration, and began shouting at him.

"I've told you that I'm only staying here because I don't have any alternative, at least not one that I can see. I've told you I don't want you, that we're never going to be married in the real sense of the word. You've accepted everything 'so that the others won't laugh.' That's what you said. What more do you want? And if—"

Without letting me finish, he grabbed my book and tried to pry it from my hands.

We fought over it briefly, and I got out of the car. Mişu then grabbed hold of my skirt so I couldn't escape.

"Help!" I started to yell, "Help, help." Two young people were passing by and one of them grabbed Mişu by the collar. But Mişu said calmly, "This is my wife."

It was only then that I realised the seriousness of my predicament, and the humiliation I was faced with. I couldn't speak English; I couldn't explain my side of the story. People had come out from nearby shops and offices to see what all the noise was about. During the fight my sandal had broken, but I still had the book, and I sat down on the curb, crying.

Somebody patted my shoulder. A lady wanted to know what had happened; but I couldn't explain. I smiled, and got up, and in my bare feet headed home. I had just sat down on the grass in front of our house, since I didn't have any keys, when a police car arrived. The young man who got out tried to find out something about what had happened, but again, because I couldn't speak English, I couldn't really tell him anything. He gave me a phone number that I understood I could call if I had problems.

Then Mişu appeared in a car with a policewoman, and judging by the look she gave me, I was sure he had given his version of events, and she believed it. I knew the story, since I had heard it so often. "She came here, I did everything for her, she lied to me, she has a lover in Australia, they're after my money." It was easy to believe, I suppose. I was forty-seven, he was seventy-six. They couldn't know what was a lie and what was the truth.

The policewoman made a hand signal to her partner which I translated as, "He's right." I couldn't defend myself. And as I'd learned, even when the truth is plain and evident, people often don't understand it or simply choose not to see it.

The police left, I turned to go into the house and it was locked. Mişu was inside, already on the phone to his friends in Australia, telling them his version of what had happened, and in very nasty language, how terrible I was.

The glass pane in the front door had been broken and taped since the day I arrived. I removed the tape now, put my hand in through the hole and pushed down on the door handle. But Mişu saw what I was doing. He put the phone down, picked up his cane and tried to hit me, following me down the step. I ran away and hid behind some bushes, from where I saw him go back to the house, come back out with a camera, and take pictures of the broken glass pieces and the hole in the window. Then I heard him calling someone on the phone. Before long, the police car appeared and the two officers from before got out.

"Look what she did," Mişu shouting and waving his arms around. "She broke the window! Look at the glass."

I came out and showed them my hands, which was all I could do to protest my innocence – they were unmarked, so it didn't look as if I had forced or broken a window.

The police wanted to come into the house, but after the first step they covered their noses, unable to stand the strong, acrid stench of the dogs and filth that by now I had become accustomed to. Mişu, ignorant of their reaction, proudly began showing them the house.

Finally I was able to get into the next door house, where I took out my suitcases, and broke down again.

"Where can I go, what can I do?" I asked the suitcases. "I want to go home, I want to leave and go home." That was all I could say, through the tears. Though bitter at Mişu, I understood that I deserved everything that was happening to me. I had made a mistake, and reality was attacking my soul.

Mişu appeared with the policemen, and I gathered that they had arranged for me to stay with Dana and Vica for a few days. I picked up my things, and again arrived at their place, which had been a refuge for me so often.

But this meant that at last the police were able to get a second opinion about Mişu. I was still upset, but couldn't help smiling when I saw the fervour with which they described him.

"He's a liar, a scoundrel, and a cheat. You can't believe

anything he says." After what they'd seen, the police understood, but that didn't do much to help me. The story threads he'd woven around me, and the legal strings he'd put in place, meant there was nothing I could do to get away easily.

Mişu showed up the next day, begging and pleading before he even got through the door. "Please forgive me. Elena, don't leave. What will people think, what will our community say?"

Nobody believed his remorse, but still I couldn't see what else I could do. I tried to at least get some admission on his part of how he had schemed and trapped me.

Once on the phone to me in Denmark he had told me, "Don't worry, I gather evidence." I didn't understand what he meant. Now I did. Words and lies and half-truths were his stock in trade. It was an unequal fight, for me to try and convince anyone, let alone the authorities in this country where I still could not speak the language, of what he had done and how he behaved. He often told me now, "You are not meant for this life and I am going to destroy you." And, "You are a fool if you think anybody is going to believe you, since everybody believes me. I know exactly what to tell them." And it was true, there were plenty of people who believed what he told them about us.

"I want you to admit in front of these people that you lied to me. That when I had finally given up on the idea of Remus coming here, that you encouraged him, you promised me all your help, you said you would pay for everything and you wanted to escape from your loneliness."

It didn't take him long. "I admit it," he said.

It was a pointless victory against someone who used words to cheat others, but hearing the truth just that once soothed my soul, confirming to me that I wasn't mad, that I hadn't fallen for lies that I had made up myself.

19

Regardless of how kind Dana and Vica were, I couldn't stay with them forever. While I was there I met their neighbour, Mrs. Coca. She was from Romania and had been living here for many years, and was interested to meet me. Mişu, insanely house-proud as usual, invited her to see where we lived. She did that, and after the tour, when she and I were together on the street, she whistled through her teeth. "Leave," she said. "Leave this pigsty immediately! How can you stay here with a child? I would get out in the street and shout, 'Help!'"

One night, around one in the morning, I heard voices in the house, and I understood somebody had come who had recently arrived from Romania. After a few minutes, Mişu appeared to tell me it was an old friend of his. Mişu called anybody who greeted him friend.

But I was eager to hear fresh news from Romania, so I dressed and, in a few minutes, came out to meet the visitor. Toni was a little over forty, tall, dark-haired, and above all very talkative. The table was already full of liquor, and the two were talking heatedly.

From what I heard, Toni had come on business, and he was looking for partners and also money, which he wanted from Mişu. He was after $20,000.

"Uncle Mişu, I know you can help me out. I need it now, at the start. This is an exceptional opportunity and we're going to expand really fast. I can even hire your sons," he said, turning to me.

I didn't think about it. I didn't know anything about business, but it sounded like a chance to have my children near me, and I didn't suspect any ulterior motives. I only wanted a way out, an escape route from Mişu, and I thought the only way for that to happen was to have my sons with me.

Within the hour, Toni called Dragos in Canada, to talk him into the job. After he had finished talking, I took the phone to find out what he thought.

"Mum, who is this guy?" he said. "Stay where you are, be calm and leave them to sort out whatever that business is. I'm coming next month to get you out of there."

I was elated. It wasn't what I had intended, but could it be that my prayers would be answered? Suddenly, it was much easier for me to put up with Mişu and his irksome presence.

It was a welcome change to have someone else in the house. It was nearly dawn when Mişu handed me a flashlight to lead Toni to the house next door while he stayed back to look for the keys. I walked carefully on the short path connecting the two houses, when suddenly I felt Toni come near and bend down, trying to kiss me. Terrified, not understanding what was going on, I withdrew speechlessly. For the first time in our 'marriage', I was glad to see Mişu appear in the dark.

This was yet another situation I had no idea how to handle; yet more behaviour I couldn't understand. Who would behave like that to a woman, supposedly the wife of someone whose help and money you were asking for? It was baffling and frightening.

In the morning I was in the kitchen when Toni appeared, a big smile on his face as if nothing had happened.

"What was that about last night?" I asked. "How can you come to somebody's house, forget about what state it's in, and be welcomed in, behave like you're his friend, and then do that? I can't understand it. Who are you and what do you want?"

He laughed, and at last seemed a little embarrassed. "I tried my luck, that's all. I promise it won't happen again. I need help to get this money from Mişu."

"Oh!" I said. "You came here to try and get his money and when you saw me, you thought I might get in the way, or might be able to help you? Is that why you tried it on?"

"Something like that," he answered.

I asked Mişu later whether he would give Toni the money he was after, and whether he thought he'd get it back.

"Oh, yes," he said. He's very genuine in that respect. I am going to give him some money, but only $5,000."

I didn't share his opinion, but it was none of my business.

Toni stayed at the house for three weeks, witnessing the daily circus and the muted struggle between Mişu and me. He reported to me all the bad things Mişu said about me, and I was certain that if I had said anything about Mişu, that would have gone directly to him. I had no control of course over anything Toni might make up. The one good thing about having a visitor in the house was that Mişu had someone else to complain to about me so I didn't have to listen to it. Then, a young woman came by one day and asked Mişu if she could stay for a few days. She was a friend of one of his acquaintances from Germany. She stayed for a week, and became friendly with Toni. Both of them kept Mişu in check, for which I was grateful.

During this time, I was visiting Dana often. That and my walks were the only way I could find any peace. Nothing satisfied me, I had no avenue for creativity, or joy, and I had no idea where to look for it. If this was a test, it was much too hard for me, I hadn't been prepared for it. I wandered purposelessly in the streets, my soul torn apart, carrying the weight of the misfortune brought about by recklessly latching onto a stranger.

After the girl left, the noisy evenings resumed. Mişu and Toni stayed up drinking every night. I wasn't surprised when one night, Mişu came into my room, foaming at the mouth and shouting, "I'm going to kill him! I'm going to kill him!"

He was talking about Matei. I couldn't calm him down and so I picked up Anca and went next door to call Toni, who had just gone to bed. I don't know what they said, but for a while it was quiet in the house. Then I heard the car engine running, and I assumed Mişu had gone out. Before long he reappeared, though, bleeding from his temple and his mouth. He had gone to get the police, apparently, then fortunately for him thought better of it and came back, only to crash the car into the garage.

"Look! It's your fault! You and that guy from Australia. You want to kill me." He raved for a while longer and then fell asleep.

Every now and then, since I had cleaned up the house next door a little, I would invite Dana and Vica to dinner. But the evening would always end badly. Mişu would start to attack his favourite subject: Matei. He complained that I talked with him on the phone, that he disliked my tone of voice, that he gave us food and I didn't want to come to his bed.

"I buy a lot of everything for her to eat and get fat, to get ugly so that guy won't want her anymore." I heard it and couldn't believe it. On another occasion, I heard him tell them, "She is my wife, even if she doesn't admit it."

I wasn't a model of patience. I felt the blood rush to my head, I couldn't stand it anymore. Rushing into the room like a whirlwind I confronted him.

"Repeat what you just said."

"I said what I said. What, do you want them to believe I am a fool? Who do you think you are, Princess Diana!?"

Not letting him go on, I hit him right in the mouth. I didn't have any other way of paying him back for all the humiliation and abuse that I had to endure daily and surely I had yet to endure. I don't know if it was true but I heard him scream, "Stop it. You've knocked my tooth out. I will keep on speaking out, I am going to tell everyone and what are you going to do? I am going to destroy you. You are not made for such a life," he kept repeating endlessly.

Blind with fury, I picked up the soup plate off the table and threw it in his face. Then I left. I took Anca, who was playing out in the street, and walked off, trying to calm down.

Toni finally left. While he had been staying, I had offered him the cleanest room in the next door house, which was where I kept my own belongings, still packed. I had also been keeping the letters I'd received from Matei – the ones I knew about – in my suitcases. I'd heard Mişu mention these to Toni, and when he left, I checked and found that they were no longer there. Also missing was some of my lingerie. They were all new items that had gone, and I could easily see what was missing. "I hope he got them for his wife," I thought to myself.

As well as intercepting my mail, Mişu kept track of who I called by using the redial button. He'd obtained Matei's number this way, and would call him every so often. Although he had little to say that wasn't abuse, he would stay on the phone for hours, and then show the bills to anyone who had time to listen. "Look, she talks for hours to Australia and I have to pay." He did the same thing with the Romanian and Danish phone numbers that I had used when I arrived to call my family and friends.

One day, coming in through the back door, I surprised him talking to Matei – if those rants of his could be called "talk."

"Because of you I got sick, I have double vision," he was shouting. A little silence and then, "I am going to kill you." Then he slammed the phone down.

"What is it," I asked him, "why do you want to kill him?

"You know what he said? He said if I see you double, then I should keep the copy and send him the original."

"Good for him! He knows what he wants."

"Yes, you side with him. I am going to destroy you. I am never going to give up."

"Do what you want." I didn't have the strength to argue with him, or even be concerned any longer by the crazy things he said.

At last Dragos' arrival day was here. I had given up caring about the way I looked, because I knew anything I wore would get dirty from coming into contact with so much rubbish every day. Now I thought I would make an effort, but I felt so much older than I had just two months ago, when I arrived full of hope and still feeling young. My nerves were stretched to the limit. I was full of shame; tear-stained, upset, restless.

Dragos looked unchanged, and Mişu put us in the car and carried out his usual tactics. He took us to nicest parts of town, talking incessantly and boasting of his family tree, which, of course, was full of generals and leading engineers.

"Tell me about some of them," I taunted him.

"What? I told you a thousand times I come from a family of generals. There were great people in my family. I am an engineer."

"And regarding the work you did, Mr. Engineer, the men that worked with you say you did a great job of washing the parts from plane engines."

"I flew, I flew. I am a pilot."

I knew he had been, although I didn't know the circumstances. I just wanted to annoy him, and by attacking his ancestry I always succeeded. In spite of his haughtiness, in everything he did you could easily see he was a base man, and I told him that without restraint.

"You're a long way from being educated," I would tell him, "but I admit that you have schooling which people like you value a lot."

"What schooling?" he asked.

"The school of deception. That's what your imperial forefathers probably did since you are so well schooled in that," I provoked him. "You'll be telling me you have Royal blood in a minute."

It was childish, and I knew it. I usually kept my mouth shut in such situations, but sometimes couldn't help letting some of my ill-feeling boil over.

At home I had arranged Dragos a clean room next to Anca's and mine. Embarrassed, I avoided showing him around the houses.

"What," said Mişu, "you don't want to show him? Are you ashamed of your own housekeeping?"

Then and over the next few days, Dragos observed everything in silence. He didn't react or respond to Mişu, which was hard for Mişu to deal with as he was so accustomed to talking his lies into truth.

He bought deli items worth hundreds of dollars, and showed everyone the receipts, "Look how much I buy and she is still unhappy." In fact he gave most of this food away, to the mechanic who fixed his car, his neighbours, his son, but that wasn't part of his story.

For two weeks he kept taking Dragos to see various houses, because, as he said, "we intend to move." I knew this was a lie, that he wasn't going to do anything, and he only wanted to build an impression for Dragos. Dragos, however, refused to believe anything.

"Mum, this man lies. He is a thief. Why do you waste your time? You must leave immediately."

I didn't argue. Together, we visited Mr. R., the immigration lawyer. During our conversation he handed Dragos a piece of paper.

Dragos read it. "This paper, or a copy of it, was given to Mişu," he said. "It shows clearly that it is not necessary to marry him in order to stay here or for Remus to be able to come. Mişu was given this paper to read to you. Do you know anything about it?"

Of course I didn't. I was flabbergasted. This evidence of Mişu's lies rekindled all my anger and self-doubt. What had I done wrong to get myself involved with such a vile man? Although vague at first, the one thought that became clearer and clearer was that I had got what I deserved.

At last, I finally took action. That same night, seeing as I couldn't get an apartment or financial assistance, I got myself into Women's Refuge accommodation.

I wasn't familiar with Wellington's districts and I found myself with Anca in a strange, remote part of town, in a meagre house that seemed to say everything about the women there. Looking at the dirty bed linen, I sat on the bed crying desperately. How did I get here? How can I get out of here? Why did I ever leave, what am I doing here? Every time I was in situations that made me ashamed, I thought of Anca who was suffering beside me. I hugged her and we crouched in a bed. These, I thought, were truly the worst days of my life.

The following day passed very slowly. Dragos was not allowed in to see me, but I was happy to go out and meet him, even if just for an hour. In the evening, I decided to take him and go to Dana's, on foot.

We set off, but after some time I had to tell him, "Dragos, I don't know where we are, but I am sure Dana lives far from here.

We can't get there without taking a bus. I am mentally exhausted, I cannot walk, it is already past eight, Anca is tired, we've got no idea where we are going. We need to get a bus."

"How can we do that? Let's try a bit longer."

After another half an hour, we were near a bus stop and one was ready to leave. Decisively, I headed for the driver. Dragos insisted, "Please, don't do that."

"Why? What's wrong?"

"I left my wallet at home. Mişu gave me a ride."

"It's okay. You can find good people everywhere," I told him and went up to the driver.

"I don't have any money, I am with a little girl, it's night-time, I don't feel well and I must get to Lyall Bay," I told him breathlessly.

I have no idea what language I was speaking. But something got across pretty clearly, because although the bus route didn't include Lyall Bay, the driver set us down as close as he could. It was nine thirty and I still had no idea where we were, so I stood in the road and signalled passing cars.

"Mum, what are you doing?"

"I am asking for help. What else can I do? I couldn't have done this alone, but with you, I am not afraid."

Eventually somebody stopped and offered to take us to Dana's house. As usual, she was kind and welcoming. "Come here and stay, we have room. You should have come from the beginning."

The next day I resolved the issue of financial aid, and by evening Anca and I had a nice apartment in a small building across from the Botanic Garden.

Mişu followed us everywhere. At each step of the journey, he was trying to change my mind. "Come back. I will sell everything, buy something new. What will people say about me?"

I said I wasn't interested in anything coming from him.

"If you became the richest man on earth, you will still be Mişu and I don't want anything to do with you."

"But I love you, I will do anything for you."

"I'm sorry."

The apartment was made up of two bedrooms, a sitting room, kitchen and bathroom. All of them were bright, roomy, clean and empty.

"It's okay," I told myself, "If I escaped that crowded slum and the misery of Mişu, now you'll see, I can do anything."

I put the suitcases down in the middle of the apartment and looked around without having any idea of how I could get hold of a bed, table, any furniture. I had nothing. Dragos had to go in two days, and now anxiety overcame me. Yet again, I felt lost in an unknown place. In the evening he came with Mişu, who, suddenly very placatory now, told me I could choose anything I wanted from him.

I remembered the Romanian saying, "It is bad with bad, but without bad it is worse." I had no choice. I brought over a bed and a torn couch that, when covered, became useful. From the Salvation Army, I got two twin beds that became a king-sized one when put together. Dana came loaded with pots and pans, plates, cutlery and glasses.

After Dragos left, every morning Mişu was at the door.

"Let me take Anca to school. Open the door."

I knew he didn't do anything without a clear goal. He wanted to be seen with Anca at school, to demonstrate how attentive he was, and at the same time he wanted to watch my every move. But as long as he didn't live with me, he didn't inconvenience me. Then fear made me accept another compromise. "Let me come and I will bring some food," he said.

With everything in my mind so unstrung, I said to myself,

"Why not? I have the key and I can open the door when I want to."

After a short while, I told him to stop taking Anca to school. He hadn't changed and was usually late, so I would get upset and he enjoyed that. I found a path through the gardens that led to the school and we used it every morning. I tried to limit Mişu's time around us as much as possible but he wasn't one to give up easily. He would knock at the door and not stop until I opened it.

"You still need me. Don't drive me away. I know you don't have enough money. I'm on my own. Just let me bring some food, and let me stay for dinner." I tried to think of what else he was after, what he wanted, and it didn't take me long to find out. Dana and Vica would visit us, and always when Mişu was there sparks would fly. Dana reproached him for having lied to me, for not being genuine. She said he had to help us and not gossip about me to anyone. I wasn't in touch with anybody, but she heard all the stories that Mişu spread about me wherever he could. Upset, she turned to me, "Don't let him in any more. Do you know what he is saying? You would blush with shame if you heard."

"He's promised to pay. He has to pay to get Remus here. Once he's here, then I'll see."

I wasn't worried about the expenses Mişu incurred. It was his choice. What pained me was the ceaseless fight between us, the hurtful situation I was in. It stirred in me a restlessness that didn't leave me for years. I was starting to worry about my health.

Remus and his wife arrived on April 16. I hadn't seen him since his brief visit to Denmark one Christmas; his wife, Lili, I had known since she was a little girl. She lived in the same town; they had been schoolmates from the elementary grades. Their paths had diverged when they went to university, but by chance they had found each other again.

My son was familiar with my circumstances, but after Mişu's

over-the-top promises on the phone I wondered how he would regard the reality. What worried me was Lili. I knew the Romanian mentality well: if you got to the West, you were automatically rich. It was inconceivable, unacceptable, to think that you could be anything other than rich. Lili was young, she dreamt, like anyone, of a good life, but she hadn't experienced hardship like I had, and so I had to be prepared for anything. The first alarm signal I had was when we returned from the airport. I could see from her face that she was unimpressed by the look of the apartment. How is she going to cope? I asked myself.

From the beginning, Mişu had taken Remus and Lili through the usual routine. He greeted them at the airport, saying, "Let me show you the letters your mother wrote to me when she was in Denmark. You should know," he added, "that she is now my wife." Finally, we wound up at his house. "See how well I live. And your mother sneers at it." Nobody answered him.

Remus avoided any discussion, but that didn't discourage Mişu, who seemed to believe if he talked loud enough, he would find enough listeners. At the end of it all Remus came away saddened.

"Forgive me for insisting that we come," he said. "It was hard to imagine how things were. It makes me so sad, to think what you must have been through with this man. But we will find a solution."

Remus and Lili quickly filed residency applications. In order to have their qualifications validated, though, Lili had to attend courses at the local university, while Remus would have to pass an exam in order to practise medicine. They weren't happy about it, but there was little they could do.

Meanwhile Mişu continued in the only way he knew how. I knew from the way he behaved while I lived in his house that he wasn't in touch with the Romanian community in Wellington. He would take any opportunity to shout that this person or that person had been a communist, a tool of the regime, a spy who reported every move of the Romanians here, which didn't win him any friends.

Now, taking a bottle of wine or a box of treats, he would visit community gatherings and spend his time discrediting me, telling everyone how I had deceived him.

By chance I discovered that he was interfering with my mail at my new apartment. Remus and I decided to catch him out. We set up camp on a bench hidden among some trees in the Botanic Garden across the street. From there we could see everything that went on in front of the building. Sure enough, Mişu soon showed up, parked the car and settled in to wait. When the mailman came by, Mişu got out to approach him. We dashed across the road and stood behind them just as Mişu was asking for the mail.

"I live at number—" He began stammering when he saw us, at a loss to explain himself.

"Go," I told him, "I don't want to see you again."

"Please understand, I didn't mean any harm." How could he say that? He simply wouldn't give up.

"Don't come to visit us, I don't want to see you."

Matei had let me know he was planning to come over for Anca's birthday. I was determined that he and Mişu should not meet, as I knew no good could come of it.

I was glad to see him, and to me he was the same; it seemed as if we had parted just a few days previously and only for a short while as we had arranged, and that now everything was normal.

The relief was just illusory. Matei had arrived with a large bottle of cognac and he proceeded to drink most of it during the three days he stayed with us. When he was drunk, fights erupted from God only knows what. As usual, I would withdraw early and go to bed. I tried to avoid the subject of Mişu, but Matei wanted to discuss nothing else. On the third night, I had fallen asleep when I was suddenly wakened by a strong blow to my body. As I struggled to understand what was going on, I felt such a strong pain in my hip I couldn't move.

Matei, drunk, had remembered that I had left him, but had forgotten why. When he was drunk, he couldn't go to bed easily. He shouted and carried on, trying to explain himself. We just wanted him to calm down, so we and the neighbours could get some sleep. But we were wasting our time. Finally, at around three in the morning, he took his bag and stormed out.

I felt I was suffocating; I was breathing heavily, panting, and then I fell down in a faint in the hallway. I came to on the couch in the sitting room, with Remus, Lili and even Anca around me, all trying to help. Anca patted my hands, Lili had a glass of water and Remus stroked my forehead.

"Mum, just hang on a little bit longer and then we'll leave together for Australia. Think! I can work there for four years before I need to take the exam. You are coming with us and it will all be fine. Everything's going to be OK," I heard him say.

I thought of what had happened, and was deeply anxious about Matei. Where did he go, in the middle of the night, when he didn't know anybody? I assumed he had left for Australia, and in a few days tried to get in touch with him. I received an ultimatum in response: "If you don't come here by July tenth, it's all over." I didn't call him back.

Mişu reappeared in a week.

"Please, please, I will bring food and I will only come in the evening for dinner." He didn't have to insist, I would have taken him in anyway. I was once again desperate. We didn't have enough money and he knew it. I was miserable, but at the same time an even stronger passion drove me. "It's not possible, it's not possible, something has to happen!" I tried to console myself with little things such as walking, anywhere, just to scatter the fog that descended on my soul every now and then.

The walks helped, even though the atmosphere I found on my return was none too bright. Remus was anxious and uneasy, and I could tell it was because he too felt helpless in the circumstances we were in. Lili, on the other hand, I sensed was jealous of the warm, close relationship between my son and me. She resented seeing us chatting, and liked it even less when we went for a walk on the street at night. I tried to explain to her, thinking of the mother-in-law/daughter-in-law relationship, that I would never represent a danger to her. I was only trying to set Remus's mind at ease. She didn't understand, and of course this situation was perfect material for Mişu Learning of the tension between us, he didn't miss the chance to take advantage. Added now to the list of crimes and misbehaviour he would tell anybody, friend or stranger, about me, was how I ruined the days for my daughter-in-law. It was easy enough for him to make up and to believe, but for the first time I was not affected by what he was saying.

One day Remus said, "Mum, I remember you saying that when you were young, you used to paint. Why don't you try that again?"

What prophetic advice this turned out to be. Somehow we found the money to buy a few materials, then I found an old book with pictures taken at the Romanian Village Museum, and I began. Remus brought me a flower to try. I remember it was very crudely done, but Remus was impressed and encouraged me to go on. Together we went to libraries or anywhere I could gather information about painting techniques. I was suddenly engrossed in picking up my old hobby, and wanted night to turn to day so that I didn't have to interrupt my work or my study. In a short while the apartment was re-decorated: an old wooden church, a Romanian interior, a still life, portraits, landscapes – I was well aware they were a very modest beginning, but I hung them on the walls, rejoicing at every step I took towards making better, more beautiful work.

In August Remus and Lili's residency permits came through, and we decided to leave for Australia. Remus had confirmed that as soon as they arrived there, he could work for four years before taking his diploma validation exam. It sounded good. Although I hadn't heard from him since his departure in the middle of the night, I was so glad to be getting away from Mişu that I called Matei to talk about our plans. I could hear that he was pleased, and that encouraged me to share my intention to go to art school and my wish to finally have a normal life. "I don't want to suffer any more," I said.

"Come over here," he said. "I don't want to suffer any longer either."

I came to life, thinking that he had the same thirst for peace and quiet that, like me, he only dreamt of. I didn't want to disregard the offer and so I believed in it, thinking that all the mistakes we had made had made us better. Had it really been a mistake to leave him? I wondered. It remained to be seen.

20

A LITTLE BEFORE THE CHRISTMAS HOLIDAYS, WE LEFT NEW Zealand. Matei greeted us, and straight away his cold, absent look struck me. He looked at me, but didn't see me – he looked through me. He was driving a car, and I asked him who had lent it to him.

"Some old people," he answered, but I felt he was lying. We stayed at his place, but he would leave, return late, and not say a word. It wasn't hard to guess that he had a girlfriend. On the other hand, he had bought a new bed and mattress for Anca, and wanted her to start school in the neighbourhood.

I was at a loss. Why had he told me to come? Why did he say he didn't want to suffer any more, then act like this? Why does he talk to me in such a way, why does he insult me? To get here we'd had to overcome every obstacle in the hope of a new beginning. How many times did we have to do this? Why does he lie? He had always lied to me, but the only time he had admitted it was in Denmark. There, in a moment of weakness, he had confirmed my suspicions: how much he had lied and cheated on me, once I had moved to live with him in the country.

I had felt it at the time, but I was too content and too busy with the life I had. All I could do was to let my discontent overflow in a few verses:

> *How long are you going to keep tormenting*
> *me?*
> *You, the embodiment of lies,*
> *What demon brought you here*
> *To my unblemished life?*

Having resident status in Australia meant I could contact the authorities in order to get child support assistance. But talking with Mihaela, our old acquaintance from Germany, I learned that before you could get a house you had to wait in a transit camp. I knew what it meant to live in such a place and I didn't want to expose Anca to that ever again. With my limited knowledge of English, I wasn't confident I could obtain any work. Moreover, although Matei was busy now, I knew that he would never let me be, especially if we lived in the same city.

To dispel any shred of peace for me, I learned that from the previous September, changes had taken place regarding New Zealand residents' rights in Australia. Only if he had been a New Zealand resident then, the year before, would Remus have had the right to work. Now he had no chance. What was I to do? History was repeating itself with Matei. There were two options for Remus and Lili: return to New Zealand or to Romania. The conflicts with Matei were stormier than ever. He insulted me as I never imagined I would ever be insulted: "I don't want you, I have never wanted you, you forced me."

Why couldn't he have said this before we came? Once again I felt overwhelmed. I was struck by a suffocating pain that clouded my mind, draining my strength, until one morning I simply collapsed on the kitchen floor. I could see no other choice but to return to New Zealand.

The next day as I was leaving the apartment building to go shopping, I glimpsed Matei in the phone booth outside. I walked up on his blind side, getting right next to the booth without his seeing me, and listened. He was telling whoever it was on the line in minute detail how he poisoned my days, and how joyful he was I had decided to leave.

It seemed I still had more to learn about how gullible and stupid I was. Matei had lied to me in countless situations when it hadn't crossed my mind that the truth could be anything other than what he was telling me. I had spent so much nervous energy and hope on something useless. I had been wrong, so long ago, to break with convention, and doing so had brought me endless misery, humiliation and argument. Then and for years afterwards I was passionate in my desire to put things back together, to make everything right that I had broken, without really stopping to think whether it was possible. It wasn't, and I'd paid the price again and again.

I waited for Matei to get out of the booth, just so he could see me.

Dana said she would be glad to put me up until I could find a place of my own. I returned to New Zealand and started to knock on every possible door in order to obtain an apartment. Mişu soon found out I was back and promised to help. I didn't know what that would look like, but as soon as I got to the council housing offices, I found out. They knew I was married and that I had left my husband to go to Australia. So thanks to these allegations, I was unlikely to get a council apartment. I tried legal means to put the story right, but they wouldn't even agree to a meeting. "Yes, we know you lived in one of our apartments. But it's not possible now. Your husband told us everything." I asked others to intervene for me, but nothing worked. I had succeeded, with Mişu's "help" in creating a bad name for myself.

Then a chance encounter at Dana's house put me on a new path. Freda, the wife of one of Vica's Romanian friends, suggested I try the government's Housing Corporation. The accommodation was more expensive, but they would find something for me eventually. It turned out to be good advice. It took a few weeks because I was after a location near Anca's school and close to transport, but finally Anca and I were in our own place.

While I was staying with Dana, after taking Anca to school I would paint. I showed some of what I was doing to Freda, who I thought had exquisite taste. She encouraged me to go to night classes for painting and even gave me paints and canvases as gifts.

Our apartment was on the fourth floor in an apartment building perched on a hill near the centre of town. To reach it, there were two options: climb the steep street uphill or take the one hundred and ninety-six steps. I hated both options, especially when I returned loaded with market bags and tired after a work day. For Anca it was ideal. The bus picked her up at the foot of the steps and dropped her off in front of the school, and then vice-versa. Dana again helped me with furniture; a bed, a table and whatever else she could find for the kitchen. Although it was very meagre, we were content. I didn't have enough money left after paying the rent, so was forced to accept visits from Mişu in return for some assistance. I knew I had to do something but still lacked the courage to get rid of him for good. I had left Australia to escape one form of suffering, and while I was now free of Matei's torment, I still felt a lack of purpose. I didn't have the courage to stop and ask myself what else I should do.

Remus and Lili had returned to Romania. I was surprised, though perhaps I should not have been, when Matei started to call me even while I was still at Dana's.

"Why did you leave?" he asked. "I would have come to my senses." Maybe he would have, but I simply couldn't have handled going down that road again.

Evenings were quiet, with no TV, no radio, no friends. I read stories to Anca, then went to bed very early. I had registered with an in-home care agency, and soon we had some more regular income. It was clear that it didn't matter how you earned your money as long as you did it honestly, and, with steady work, we started to be "rich", as Anca put it.

Then I had a piece of luck. The agency sent me to meet an old woman who needed care. Valerie was a painter: her walls hung thick with portraits, figures that seemed ready to talk to you. She was old and moved slowly, but her love of painting hadn't diminished and she still held classes for those wishing to capture human faces on canvas.

I showed her one of my works, and she invited me to her Tuesday afternoon classes. It wasn't easy to get there; all day I was on the run from bus to bus. But I didn't want to miss such an opportunity. I learned the basics of portrait painting and got along very well. Valerie would often come and sit next to me, and we'd try to put together a meaningful conversation despite my struggles with the English language.

"Do you think there is anything after death?" she asked me once.

I could tell she was worried. And one day she said, "I don't want to die in an old people's home. Would you ask for my entire house if you took care of me?"

"No. But I would be happy to live there without paying rent." She liked the idea and we decided to clean up her house. In the meantime, she suggested I leave the agency and work with her privately.

Cleaning up meant painting the walls, windows, doors and

trim. It was no small job, and Valerie asked someone she knew, John, to come and help. Things looked good; I was happy to be living there because I wouldn't have to run from bus to bus, and I would have the chance to develop my art under her direction.

"You are very kind," John told me one day. "Valerie loves you." It was a nice thing to say, but something gave me the feeling not to trust him.

One day I prepared lunch for Valerie as usual, and with the tray set I headed for the studio where on sunny days she liked to eat, then rest.

"Let me take it," John said, "It's no problem." He took the tray off me and went to serve Valerie.

A few days later John came into the room where I was painting the trim. He asked me how much an hour I was working for. Naively, I said, "Fifteen dollars."

"Okay, but my rate is forty dollars. And I'm not working in such a hurry. I don't understand why you are in such a hurry."

I realised he was seeing me as competition, and he didn't like it. But what troubled me most was that John was talking more and more with Valerie behind closed doors. Something was going on, but what? As I was tidying up the house, I would check every item. Good things I left where they were; anything I considered too worn or used I would place in a bag, which I put in a corner of the garage.

"I hope you didn't toss anything out," Valerie said one day. I told her what I'd done, and that she could find two bags in the garage. Then a few days later she asked to see them. To my astonishment and despair, the bags were gone.

I asked John if he knew where they were. He smiled and said, "I threw them out, since that's what you asked me to do."

The next day, when I arrived at Valerie's house, John came to the door. "Valerie said she doesn't require your services any longer."

I couldn't believe it. Although he was blocking my way, I got round him to try and speak to her. "What's going on?" I asked. "What's happened?"

"Didn't you hear what she said?" John's voice came from behind me. "Out!"

I had worked honestly and hard – harder than John. Why had this happened? I could see John had poisoned Valerie's mind against me, but why should that happen, just when things seemed to be going well?

I left the house crying, upset at this injustice, but also because I was so worried for Valerie. On the footpath I bumped into one of Valerie's friends. She had witnessed the whole thing, and interceded for me. "Valerie, how can you do this after everything Elena has done for you? What lies has this man told you?"

But Valerie didn't say a word. So I left, and never saw her again. I learned through the friend that a few months later she had found out the truth about John. For the slightest service performed, fixing a skirt hem, repairing a chair, small odd jobs, he charged her thousands of dollars. He cashed cheques she signed after he served her a few glasses of cognac. She finally sent him away, but a short while after fell sick and was hospitalised in a nursing home, where she eventually died. My own misfortune aside, I wondered what had she done to deserve that? Why does such misfortune show up, and blight the lives of good, honest people?

Fortunately, with the help of some kind people, I was able to find more work, and I was again earning a decent living. But Mişu was still out there, and he wouldn't waste any opportunity to hurt me. This bothered me, as I was hurt by the continual untruths he directed against me, and because I couldn't react or defend myself.

He used to come by and, since I had decided I wasn't going to open the door to him, he would leave hanging on the door handle a bagful of rotting food. I would toss these into garbage disposal bin by the entrance to our apartment. One time he saw me do this and desperately ran to the building supervisor to ask him to open the basement door, so he could recover it.

After that he came very infrequently, and would stand outside the door screaming as loudly as he could, "I spent $150,000 on you, you took everything from me, you tried to kill me with that guy from Australia and now you leave me."

He wouldn't leave until he finished everything he wanted to say, all in English, for the benefit of the neighbours.

Then, to Anca's and my joy, Dragos and Carmen invited us to Canada for the Christmas holidays. I could hardly sit still, waiting for the days to pass. I think that helped give me the impetus to take the ultimate step to break my relationship with Mişu, and I filed for divorce. That done, we left for Canada and the promise of joy, laughter and snow. All of these we found there, and it was truly like a breath of fresh air after what seemed like so long in the darkness.

But beauty doesn't last for ever, and when we returned home I found I was dissatisfied with everything. I had always thought of myself as adaptable, and that only increased my unease. What was wrong? Like anybody else I wished for a life that would be, if not comfortable, at least normal. I couldn't see that happening in the foreseeable future. Was that why I was unhappy? Suddenly, I realised I needed friends, close friends who were aligned to my own soul's yearning, and I didn't have any. I didn't know anybody that I could consider a friend. I was Romanian, I thought and felt Romanian, and I desperately needed somebody to understand me. I wanted more than the cordiality, of the smiling but fake "Je suis désolée" that had been so much part of my suffering.

But I avoided the Romanian community. I had gone to the Romanian church in the December of my arrival in the country, at Mişu's insistence. There I met many local big-wigs, including Jean's former wife. They all looked at me as if I didn't speak their language. Since then, I had avoided any contact with Romanians, other than Dana and Vica and their friends. But I'd also had to steer clear of English speakers. I was upset by the customary, "How are you?" I knew I could say anything but the truth. Who would have had time to listen to me when I would have been unable to discuss anything other than my problems? But it was hard for me to invent that "anything." So how could I build a friendship?

In addition, I seemed to have lost the ability to sustain a conversation, even in Romanian. I preferred writing to talking. I had lost my self-esteem, and I thought that everybody looked at me as if I was some kind of vagrant. I was convinced that due to the actions of years ago, I had lost people's respect. I suffered knowing that people forget whether you are rich or poor, but they don't forget your behaviour; that the only thing that remains after you is the impression you leave behind, the honour of your name.

I needed to go to a dentist, and somebody gave me the name of a female dentist of Romanian nationality. I knew that would help when it came to understanding what was going on, so took the hint and made an appointment. When I showed up, I found a small Romanian community: the dentist, Ioana; her husband, a doctor; her mother, Mihaela, who served as the receptionist; and her aunt, also Ioana, who was the clinical assistant. Although cautious, I warmed to them. I felt a desperate need to tell somebody *the truth*, not just Mişu's fabrications. Mişu continued to stop anybody who was willing to listen to him, and it was painful knowing there were so many fans of cheap thrills. Mişu generously offered these for free.

"Pray," Mihaela told me. "God is the only hope. You will see He is going to help you."

I believed in God but I didn't pray. I didn't believe in miracles, and I didn't know how to start praying, what to ask for. I had so many needs, I felt like a beggar. But my biggest doubt was, "Do I deserve to be helped?" I had done wrong, and I caused so much wrong around me. Am I worthy of forgiveness? These were the thoughts that tormented me.

During this period, I had three dreams within a short interval. In the first, I was walking on a swampy, snowy road, looking for a less difficult and clearer path. It was hard, tiring, and at some point, in front of me rose a gigantic building. I started to circle round it, measuring its height with my eyes. On my shoulder, I carried a very long sack and I struggled hard with it – but then I realised that it wasn't heavy at all. Dragging it along behind me, I started to climb a very narrow spiral ramp that wrapped around the building. I reached the first floor. I opened a door in front of me and entered a room that struck me with its richness and beauty. Everything was gilded, everything shone. There were two people in the room, but I didn't dare show myself. I stayed hidden. Suddenly the door behind me burst open, and some invisible force came into the room. The couple I had found there disappeared and I heard someone telling me, "Look, this has been prepared for you."

That was nice, but while I held onto hope, I didn't see what I could do to change the circumstances I was in. It wasn't as if we were starving, but I couldn't reconcile myself to the thought that I was so poor, that I couldn't offer Anca and myself the chance for a life in which, in addition to everyday worries and sadness, there could be at least a little satisfaction for the soul. I suffered for Anca, who was frustrated by the lack of so many things that she should have had. I suffered for having accepted the work that I did, but it had never crossed my mind that it would be long-term. I had accepted everything as transitory, remembering the Romanian saying, "Once I slept on my beautiful bed, now I sleep on the bare ground." The thought that there was something else I had to do would not leave me. I had known good times, and I felt terrified that they would never return. I remembered my father would tell us, "Remember! It is once in a lifetime that the sea turns to honey." I couldn't accept that idea. I had to find a path. "Could it be the one I've already caught a glimpse of?" I asked myself. Maybe, but I wasn't sure yet, and anyway I was aware that it would take a long time to go along that route.

In the second dream, I was walking along a sunny, warm street, busy with people. I saw a woman, crouched by the corner of a building, holding a child. She had been crying and she didn't lift her head. I drew closer to ask if she needed help, but she disappeared and in front of me opened a huge door, like those on warehouses and factories. I entered and found myself in an immense grotto traversed by tunnels, some long, some short, branching out like the arms of an octopus. Although it was dark, I could make out countless hollows dug into the stone walls, where men and women were living in filthy conditions. Dirty hay served as bedding, and I was particularly struck by the appearance of the men: grubby, clad in rags, with ugly faces and each carrying a knife which they used to threaten their victims. It was crowded and I could see more and more people appearing from the darkness, all as dirty, and all with the same indecent and sadistic sneer.

I turned back; the door was open, I could see the sunlight outside and I could see coming from that light and slipping into this hell were girls, young women, beautiful, fair and dark, joyful and ignorant of what was in store for them. And at the same time I saw the impatient looks of those waiting for them.

I looked at myself. I was elegant, clean, and I wondered what I was doing here. Then I noticed that although I walked among them all, they couldn't see me. "What will happen if anyone sees me?" I asked myself, terrified. I wanted to get out. But now the gate was closed, and suddenly I felt myself being pushed into one of the cavities in a wall. "Stay here until the gate is opened," a voice told me. Then a curtain was drawn to block the entrance and cover me.

I ran to the phone to tell Mihaela and Ioana this latest vision. "Have hope, Elena, you are protected!" they said. I told myself, again, I wasn't worthy. Who was I, what had I done to deserve protection?

Then a few nights later came the third dream.

I was next to a priest who sat on a chair beside me, holding me, restraining me. People appeared in front of him, waiting to be judged. There was a queue, and I couldn't see its end. I understood that most of them were destined to go to a place nobody wants to go to. Among them I could see a man who seemed kind and on whose face I could see regret. I drew closer and asked him, "How did you get here? What did you do?"

"I have sinned, madam."

"What kind of sins did you commit?" But at that moment the priest drew me to him and I couldn't hear what the man said.

What could all these dreams signify? Should I hope? It wasn't enough not to act in a certain way. "Something has to be done," I kept repeating to myself, thinking that it wouldn't be normal to have everything served up on a silver platter.

The need for money had me in a tight corner. The dentist, friend though she was, had to be paid, and I had paid only half of what I owed. Where could I get the other half? I hate to borrow money, and anyway I didn't know anybody ready to help me. Dana was the only kind-hearted person I knew, but she had no money.

I had painted a few canvases with Romanian themes, one of them inspired by a landscape I had sketched in Canada. One day my friend Deborah came for a visit. She was a great admirer of all things Romanian, and sitting down at the table she took some money out of her purse. In an excited voice she told me, "Look, I have $600 for three of your paintings. Are you willing to sell them to me for that?"

I couldn't believe it. God, you really exist! It was a miracle, and one I hadn't hoped for. I was still an apprentice, and it showed in everything I did, but among my works every now and then something good popped up, and to my good fortune somebody had noticed and appreciated them. Could this be the way I should have followed? Suddenly, life didn't seem as dull any more.

At Easter, Matei visited. He was determined to take us to Australia with him.

"I am not leaving until I get my citizenship," I said. "I have suffered so much, and to just leave now? No." Fortunately, he took me at my word, and returned alone.

In May, I got the paper formalising the dissolution of my marriage to Mişu. In the same month I filed for citizenship. I was feeling better now, more hopeful. I spent my time working and painting. The autumn winds had started and I loved to watch the foamy waves struggling against rocks on the seashore, or to go for a drive through the city at night. Ioana took me on these trips whenever she could.

One day I was at home and was walking to the phone when suddenly a strange heat flooded me from my shoulders to my heels. The experience lasted for a few seconds. I had no idea what it was, only that it didn't feel like a medical problem. A few days later, in the same place, that hot arrow pierced my body again. This time, in my left ear I heard a voice saying, "Write it."

I was mystified. I had been thinking of writing something;

could it be a reference to that? I wondered. And if so, who or what is urging me to do it?

Five months had passed since I had filed for citizenship. I should have received a response by then, and was not surprised when Mr. R. informed me that, following some complaints, I wouldn't get it approved. Inquiries were being made, he said. It was ridiculous. I was an honest person working honestly to raise my child, and from the time I arrived I had done nothing wrong except fight Mişu's provocations.

In my immigration file there were one or two papers, both attesting that I had no police record. Surely they couldn't be listening to anything Mişu said? Would that man never stop plaguing me?

"Elena," Mr. R tried to calm me down, "it's their duty to make inquiries even if it is an anonymous complaint."

"No. I can't understand how some people are paid to waste time on senseless things springing from hatred without any written evidence. When you are convinced that what you are doing is right you have courage and say everything openly. Let him demonstrate that what he says is true. Why do they go along with anonymous letters? No, please get me a hearing," I asked the lawyer. "I think I have the right to defend myself."

I did get a hearing at the Ministry for Internal Affairs, where I learned what had happened. The plaintiff was one of Mişu's sons, the one who owed him the twenty thousand dollars. Without a job, and with a debt to his father, he had plenty of time to call and inform on somebody whom he had only ever briefly met a long time ago.

The information was that I lived on prostitution, but the fact the Ministry was more concerned about was that Matei had been a spy. Where, when, and for whom he had worked was not known but he was a spy for sure and they had made inquiries.

In the meantime I had heard that Mişu had called Romania as well, trying to tell my parents the same lies. They had hung up on him – I don't know whether they believed him or not. Using the phone bills from the two months I lived in his house, he called everyone I'd called in Romania or Denmark. I remembered how sure of himself he was when he said, "I am going to destroy you. They are going to believe me. I know what to tell them, you don't."

He was wrong, I realised, because it wasn't he who was destroying me. I wasn't challenging him. I let him do as he pleased. If I suffered it wasn't because of anything he said. It was because I fought against myself and my inability to remain indifferent to his taunts. I disappointed myself.

Mişu continued to dog me, or rather the people I met. He followed them home and stopped them, trying to convince them I was totally devoid of a moral compass. Some listened to him, others excused themselves, but it wasn't easy with somebody like Mişu who was the type of person who came in through the back door if you shut him out the front door. I had begun to be very careful to protect myself from his thirst for revenge.

Given his conviction that the Romanian priest in Wellington was a former security agent I was surprised to hear that now he was a regular at the church and was even on close terms with the priest. Mişu, who wasn't afraid of calling anything holy rubbish, was the last person with an interest in cultivating his soul – even though this would have been quite appropriate and praiseworthy at his age. He would bring people a gift from his boxes of drinks, trying to buy an understanding smile when he talked about me. Many of those among whom he had told tales about me had made their own mistakes, but they had known how to keep their family, and for that reason, I felt, they looked down on me. I remembered the words of one of my father's friends, "You can be totally honest, but if I come and say bad things about you, it will take time and it will be hard for you to prove you are blameless." I was in that situation now.

We got our New Zealand passports. I didn't feel any joy, though, not any more. It was not that I had become permanently discontented. But I had suffered needlessly for it, wrongfully, in my opinion. I had had a year of stress and anxiety caused by someone who lacked the courage to say out loud what he blamed me for; a year during which I saw that evil can defeat you easily and at any time if you let yourself be defeated.

And it can be so tempting to give up! Here in New Zealand where I lived the unhappiest days of my life, I remembered the dedication written on the first page of the New Testament and Psalms directing me to Psalm 51. Here after years of searching and darkness, I understood its significance. You need faith in God, faith that justice is on your side, courage and perseverance.

Everything was as it should be. That was my understanding now. I worked, looked after Anca, painted, read, and started to write. I carried a notebook everywhere I went, where I wrote down quick thoughts that came to me and that I didn't want to forget; thoughts about people, life, everything surrounding me, thinking that every one of them would at some time be useful. My basic book was now the Bible.

In Ecclesiastes, I reached the passage where it was written, "When you make a vow to God, do not delay in paying it, for he has no use for fools."

I had done exactly that. I had done it foolishly, without thinking. I had played unknowingly with serious things, and had lost control over my actions. God had withdrawn His grace and left me adrift in the material world.

There were still days of desperation, but though it was hard I tried to lift myself, to not let discouragement overwhelm my being, overwhelm and maim my soul. I remembered some lines from the

Romanian poet George Coşbuc and wrote them on a piece of paper, which I taped to the refrigerator:

> *Struggle!*
> *Life is struggle, so struggle*
> *With love and longing for it.*
> *On whose account? You are a rascal*
> *If you don't have a decisive goal.*
>
> *No matter how the struggle may end,*
> *Keep on struggling because it's your duty.*
> *They live, those who agree to struggle,*
> *And the cowards, they complain and die*
> *Should you see them dying, let them die,*
> *This is their destiny.*

Yes, struggle, but be prepared for it; that was something I hadn't known. Now I was aware that the peace and rest I craved couldn't be earned without ceaseless struggle.

I had long phone conversations on these and other religious subjects with Ioana, one of my friends. I was amazed by my discovery, and wanted to share the many thoughts that flooded me and the even more numerous questions. I had lacked in Christian guidance, and thought that this had been one of the reasons, among others, for my straying. I understood things which I had never thought I would find a meaning to.

Now I could accept the suffering and challenges I had gone through. I had been given suffering, like anybody else for that matter, and at the same time I had received, also like anybody else, the desire to free myself from it. I saw life as ephemeral, fragile, painful and, especially, unfair, and so I thought that everything would be meaningless unless there was something else.

Somewhere there has to be justice, I thought. I read that everything was created and then gifted for our use; so when did the long chain of our suffering start? I read, I sought everything I believed might make things clear to me. Who gave me my mind, how did my power to understand things change, even though in my soul I stayed the same? Who gave us feelings, hatred, love; how did we get conscience? How were they planted in our souls, from where did they spring? Questions, many questions, the answers to which I wanted right away.

I had met a lady, Caitlin, who had a property beside the sea, an hour away from Wellington. She invited Anca and me to spend the weekend there. It was a wonderful chance to see something else of this huge village common/animal pasture that was New Zealand. On our way, contemplating the hills and green, sunny fields, I realised spring was coming, the season for hope, for internal renewal. My heart warmed thinking of its imminent arrival. As the playwright T. Muşatescu said, "Spring doesn't come, it breaks out." I saw it as young, playful and bold, eager to rummage inquisitively through any corner of one's soul, taking everything out into the sunlight and spring wind, onto the green. I opened my blouse as if to invite it in: "I have nothing to hide – I am happy!"

It was as if I had gained new strength, and I began to feel that my spontaneous soul had found itself. I think our souls were moulded equally, back then, in God's fresh world; good, innocent and all alike, all equal. But along the way we lost ourselves. We were left free and we did wrong. A few of us still keep gathered inside us, unaltered, not only a tumultuous spirit but also candour, truth, courage and honesty. How wonderful it would be if we tried to find joy not only in important events, but in anything which at the time seems insignificant. What a pity that most often we waste our days in trifles that give us no satisfaction, that make us feel

stuck deeper in the mud from where you need strength to rebel
and get out with your soul untainted.

I recited verses slowly to myself, and tried desperately –
desperate because of my inability – to translate for Caitlin
something of the beauty of a few lines:

> From the first blades of grass and flowers
> I will make me a lyre with light strings
> To play, hanging on a ray of sun
>
> Because I so long for song on nature's
>   strings,
> For falling asleep rocked in a forest bed
> On branches of light shining azure...."

At the beach I ran around with Anca, amazed by the feeling of
vast openness, and at the same time by the peace and quiet around
us, which we craved so much. Anca loved the large pool near the
house, and I headed for the beach. As always I looked for nature,
nature which in its kindness seemed to prompt me to accept its
help, seeming to know my wish to get rid of dark, anxious
thoughts.

The house was the last one on a road leading to the ocean, and
from the yard a path meandered to the beach that, most of the day,
was deserted. I undressed completely and stretched out on the
sand, feeling a sensation of freedom that made my soul leap with
happiness. Everything around was silent and wildly beautiful. You
lost contact with the surrounding world just listening to the roar of
the waves, and you seemed to be urged to meditate. I looked
around; there was nobody, nobody but me, the water and the sky.
An indifference towards everything came over me, but at the same
time the sensation that I loved everybody and I could do anything.

I felt freed from all life's hardships. I found myself shouting with all my might, "God, I thank you, I thank you for the tears and suffering that brought me closer to you. I thank you and please don't leave me!"

I believe that's what we feel when we are born, but we cannot know it. It is only then that your soul can be so clean, only then you don't know what worries are, what fears are. I had forgotten everything: no children, no Canada, no Australia or Matei or Mişu. Nothing. I felt God heard me and I feverishly begged him not to abandon me, and to offer me more of these moments that reminded me that you can live some other way, other than in chains, tense with the fear of Mişu's intricate fabrications. I loved everything around me: everything was so perfect in its wild beauty, and it seemed that everything had been lovingly given to me to keep and to care for.

Finally, now, I could think and act and live in freedom.

21

I HAD REALLY KNOWN THIS LIFE; I HAD SEEN IT AS BEING FULL of bitterness and countless problems, of ups and downs; and I understood that I had the freedom to decide. At the same time a good decision requires a clear mind and an untroubled soul. My mind and soul had been overshadowed by illusion and confusion, and I still wondered if I had recovered completely.

I had needed help so badly and nobody had heard me. When you are upset, desperate, when you lose all hope, a craving fires up in you for something your intuition says is outside of yourself. I had learned you shouldn't expect help from people, not from a Jean or a Mişu or whatever else they might be called. Now I turned to the One I should have gone to from the beginning, to expect appropriate help. Unfortunately, I had only understood this so late.

Why did all this happen to me? I had asked myself. I thought how important it was to teach children as much as possible from early childhood, to make it easier for them. How important it was to be spiritually prepared when you are sent out to fight! How important it was to be taught, and then the only thing left for you to do was to go on learning by yourself. I looked back on everything that had happened, and I realised how much we were helped, or "carried," as Carmen said during a conversation we had on this theme while in Canada. I don't think we would have been able to get through our hardships without this mysterious and incomprehensible help.

While my children *believed*, I strayed on strange paths, and the moral effect of my straying was, as I have tried to describe it, fear, restlessness, distrust in myself and everybody else.

I made a mistake! And for a long, long time, regret and remorse tormented me. I was urged to forget, to get on with life. That's easy advice to give. We do carry on as the experienced soldiers that we become with time, but we can never forget what happened. On the other hand, consciously or not, we human beings do often forget the price we must pay and what we must pay it for, hoping the price will not be higher than we expected.

But there is no one to bargain with. Our conscience scolds us, and when we heed it we realise we are ashamed of some of our actions, and we want to hide them, to cover them with others we can be proud of. But we delude ourselves if we think we can forget them. I put too much heart and soul into things to be able to forget the price of my mistakes. I wasn't happy, I couldn't find peace of mind after acting against laws so simple and natural. I created too much unhappiness for those around me. Can you build happiness on others' unhappiness?

I didn't want to think of the past anymore, but I have to confess I couldn't curb my fears for the future. I had glimpsed a path and I was resolute to walk on it. I was aware it wasn't going to be strewn with flowers, but I had learned that happiness and unhappiness flow together in swift waves and what counts most is to have a goal you must fight for.

I decided to go to Canada. Getting the papers in order for that took almost two years. In the meantime, we moved to the house where we had spent such a perfect weekend. Caitlin's family only came on weekends; the rest of the time I was by myself. This gave me the chance I'd been longing for, to free myself from the stress I had lived under. I painted, biked in the surroundings, learned to drive, and started to go to clothing stores again. It felt like living in a dream. I no longer felt locked up as if in a menagerie, overwhelmed by fear. I no longer felt helpless and good for nothing. I had again started to laugh heartily, with that catching laughter that invites others to join in. I had started to sing and though my mental state was so much more optimistic, I still preferred those romantic songs that are so specific to the Romanian's natural warmth.

I learned my mother was suffering from cancer and there was no chance of her recovering. It is hard to describe my grief, especially knowing I didn't have the means to get home. I wanted so much to hold and kiss her hands, to kneel and say, "Forgive me", to quench the longing that for years had lain in her soul and mine.

Sad and restless, I went to look for a photo that I felt I had to find. Rummaging through my years of documents, I stopped to look at a scrap I had carried ever since I left home, and on which a few verses were written. The author was unknown to me but I had liked the verses and now they appeared for the first time, after so long, as if that had been their destiny:

You don't know you are still in front of me
Although you're long lost to me, my
    beloved.
The smile, vanishing among snowflakes,
You flashed at me, for one moment,

And your lock of hair tousled in the dance
   of the wind

With just my eyes I gently caressed.
The drawing of your flight on this earth
Has been erased by wind and rain,
But the moment is alive, here it is!

During the eighteen months it took to get my visa for Canada, Matei visited us a few times. As ever, fights would break out, and they convinced me we would never be together again. He insisted he would come to Canada, but not before he visited Romania. I understood our paths were separated forever, though for Anca's sake I would have liked him somewhere close to us.

Years previously, just after Matei and I moved to Mircea, I had had a dream I had never thought of again. Now every detail came back to me as if it was happening for real. I was in a carriage driven by Ion. After a while, he changed direction and disappeared. Matei was now driving the carriage, but I only stayed with him for a short period, after which he also disappeared. Now, the carriage was driven by a stranger wearing a huge hat that shadowed his entire face. Together we started to climb a mountain. On the way we passed over three obstacles. Each time I felt the shock and strength of the jolt; each time it seemed my whole being was jarred by the impact. Close to the top, I noticed I was alone; the man beside me had disappeared. I was at the top of the mountain contemplating the unmatched beauty of the surroundings, and suddenly I felt that I was floating down, losing myself in that dream landscape. At that point, I said to myself, "Now, I am dying." I woke, still feeling the jolts from the carriage in my body.

Not long before I got the visa, Dragos gave me the sad news that my mother had passed away. I hadn't seen her for thirteen years and I would never see her again. I felt a mad desire to call to her all the time. "Mother! I long to see you, to hear your lovely laugh. I want to put my head in your lap, to feel your hands caress me. Mother! You didn't want to die; you didn't want to leave your flowers, your garden and us. I can't believe you left before we could see each other again. Oh, God," I shouted desperately, "please, take care of her soul. I angered her to death; comfort her, please. She left with a soul grieving that she couldn't see me anymore."

Out of my heart-breaking pain sprang a few lines, with no literary value but which came from my soul; they were its screams of pain:

> On your death, I wish to tell you
> How much I long for you,
> For your eyes, that longingly,
> I know, were cast towards me.
>
> I left your side.
> I don't know what drove me
> To choose, instead of your love,
> A distant shore.
>
> You couldn't stop me
> Although you wanted to, I know quite well,
> And the great misery that came
> Separated me from you.
>
> It drove me to far away places
> And kept me afar,
> Far from the land where
> You rest in your death.

In autumn, hopeful and happy now that this sad, frustrating and humiliating chapter of our life was over, we left for Canada, this time sure this was the Promised Land. We left with our spirits rich in peace. I will be free, I thought. I will have time to think, I will paint, I will live unfettered by worries and fearful thoughts.

This laughter, merriment and hope accompanied us for precisely two months.

Since that first awful meeting years ago, I had never seen Carmen's parents again. I could accept they would never like me, it didn't bother me any longer. But what I did worry about was that they didn't like my son. They had never approved of Carmen's choice, and had quite openly said they wanted something else, something better for their daughter.

So I was surprised, and full of doubt, when I learned that Carmen's mother was coming to Canada to take care of the house when their child was born.

In their house, Anca and I had bedrooms downstairs, and in a corner of the living room I would paint. Carmen and her mother, Maria, would come and go without saying a word to me, as if they didn't see me. It hurt me to see Maria trying through various cheap ruses to win Dragos over. Meanwhile, I was looked on with hatred; Maria did everything short of saying, "Leave."

As usual I would overextend myself in gestures of kindness, but unfortunately my behaviour, although natural, wasn't appreciated. I tried to get Carmen aside, to remind her how much we had been through together, the hardships we had endured. Through all that we had been side by side. She acknowledged all this, how it had been between us, and yet her behaviour didn't change.

It was incomprehensible. I knew that when Carmen returned from work, Maria would fill her with lies about what I'd been doing. She did everything with a specific objective: to remove me.

ELENA MIHAILA

"I came here to maintain the household and take care of the children," Maria would say. She didn't have to speak the implied question to me: "Why did you come?"

Finally, through a series of undesirable and unpleasant events, Carmen agreed the best thing for everyone was for her mother to return to Romania.

Soon after she left, everything went back to normal. It was just us: joyful, understanding of one another and always ready for a new undertaking.

And one day Dragos and Carmen came to me and said, "We think we should return with you to New Zealand. We want to have land, we want a gentler climate, and there are other reasons why we think this is the best thing for us to do."

I was surprised, but I was also glad. I liked Canada, but from my arrival it somehow struck me as being unsuited to me. Everything seemed immense: the buildings, the cars, the stores. Of course, that wasn't reason enough to want to leave, but there was something about the place that seemed as if civilization had reached into every corner. The scale of New Zealand seemed to better suit me. There were fewer threats to your privacy, it felt like, and it was a quieter place to live with Anca.

In a year we were back, ready to start a new life, and this time to stay.

EPILOGUE

I HAVE TRIED TO CONVEY HERE THE LIFE EXPERIENCES AND events I went through with the same intensity as when they occurred and when we lived through them.

Those years of suffering and of deep soulful experience were a time of real schooling in life. I look at the wrinkles on my face now and it seems that each one reminds me of obstacles overcome with more or less ease or difficulty, of my fight against prejudice, of the turmoil of my soul. I didn't think I would find a solution to all of these. The fight against misunderstanding, against lack of interest, against ill-will, maliciousness, deceit, was the fight for our very existence.

It was hard for me to see a way forward sometimes, to see a possibility of surviving or escaping the storms that seemed to come one after the other, with the weak powers I had to resist, if not to prevail. It was hard especially when I was granted no respite, and when it seemed to me I could only escape through compromise. It would have been easy to take refuge in a so-called "diversion" – drinking, or the caresses of others. But I was waiting for help from a world whose existence I suspected, and in which now I believed. Although temptation is great, fear of and faith in God help to sustain you. I didn't have a lot of evidence of this world, but the experiences I had lived through were enough to give me the strength to do what is good and wise.

Life had taken me and shaken me in its hands to open my eyes. And although I believed at the time I was alone in the fight, now, looking back, I understand that all along I was guided, helped, and that all the time an invisible presence accompanied and protected me.

A lot of what I have said here has probably been said or written before. But I discovered it in my daily experience, and to me it seemed new and precious.

I cannot forget the past, it will always be alive and painful, and I cannot help thinking of what I went through. Everything has to be earned; you cannot sit idly. That's why I will press on, thinking of what I might need to do to regain the goodwill of fate. Although at times disheartened, I have always trusted my star and I keep looking, hoping to see it shine victoriously.

I could say that life is a big adventure upon which you should embark extremely well prepared. It is one way to say that I had to live and to suffer to become a mature person. Like a fan of mystery stories, I tried to make sense of life, but in the end I understood that I had to stand aside, that in front of me was something impenetrable, and that the wisest thing to do was to reason like a peasant – simply – and to understand that our entire universe is supported on that wise and balanced sign of the Cross, on Hope, and on Love.

SPERATE MISERI
(*In misery, hope*)

AFTERWORD

I feel that it would only be right to fulfil the reader's natural curiosity about how our lives unfolded after the final words of this work.

Upon returning to New Zealand, Anca and I returned to the same residence which we had left when we moved to Canada and there we discovered the same warmth and understanding with which we had always been surrounded.

Shortly afterwards, Dragos and Carmen also arrived in New Zealand and before too long they settled in a home on four hectares of land north of Wellington. Both worked as accountants with Dragos then pursuing a passion to become self-sufficient while also together they opened and ran a Romanian/Italian-inspired restaurant, with great success. In later years, the construction of a major road nearby brought the close of one chapter and the opening of a new stage in their lives as they moved further down the Kāpiti Coast and sought new endeavours. Their two daughters pursued their individual passions either through university study or work.

Remus and his wife also joined us in New Zealand a few years later. They bought a house and large orchard. Remus decided to complete four years of study with a notable homeopath in India and is now kept busy both by homeopathy and his orchard. His wife is employed in a veterinary line of work. Their daughter is at university.

Anca and I eventually moved to our own home near Dragos and Carmen. Anca studied English literature and French at Victoria University of Wellington and became an English teacher at her beloved college on the Kāpiti Coast. She later met her husband-to-be at a Romanian Christmas church service. They are happily settled on the Kāpiti Coast where Anca continues teaching and her husband runs his dental practice. They have recently started a family and have a young daughter.

New Zealand finally afforded us peace. I live near all my children, and we frequently meet and, as always, plot and make plans in pursuit of the next adventure or bright idea.

I am content. I am content because I have achieved what I hoped and fought for: to have my children near me. There are times when I recall all that has passed, and I feel a sense of sadness, but then I remind myself that human beings were made to be good and that we must strive therefore to be good and to not do harm to ourselves or to others. Certainly, I had encountered ill-will. Some individuals tried their best to intentionally thwart me, while others did so unintentionally in the belief that they were helping me. I have forgiven them, from my heart, and have hoped, in turn, to be forgiven.

In the last few years, I had two experiences which gave me genuine peace.

After many years, when my father died, I succeeded at last in returning home, home to my own country, for a visit. I settled myself in the house which I had deserted more than thirty years earlier. I found it alone, abandoned, but I felt happy and was pleased to notice that every inch of it, both inside and out, had been preserved exactly as I had left it.

It was summer, very hot, and I had fallen asleep in the warmth of the sun's glow that filtered through the large windows. I do not know how long I slept, but as I partially opened my eyes, next to my bed and standing before me, I saw my mother quietly watching me. Upon fully opening my eyes, I noticed that she appeared indistinct as though veiled in a delicate mist and at once she withdrew and faded from sight. I mentioned the encounter, this vision, to our priest who told me, "It is very simple. She knew you had come home, and she wanted to see you. She is happy."

Recently, for the first time since he departed this world, in a dream I met my former husband, Ion. He stood a small distance from me and looked at me with a gentle smile. From his eyes emanated goodness, understanding and a lot of love. I drew closer to him and embraced him, all the while knowing that he, too, had forgiven me.

I have found my peace.

I thank God for every trial set before me as each one has taught me and shaped me and, most importantly, I am grateful that at every turn He was there to guide, to help and to protect me.

Over the years, in the wake of the experiences I had, I finally understood that which many others perhaps have already comprehended, which is that in this world there exist laws, Divine laws, laws unwritten, laws that ought not to be forgotten and certainly not to be broken.

ABOUT THE AUTHOR

Elena Mihaila was born in Romania where she qualified as an agricultural engineer. She worked as an accountant while starting a family before making the dangerous decision to leave her homeland during the time of the Romanian revolution.

She now lives in a small town in New Zealand where she enjoys painting, tending to her garden and chickens and being surrounded by her children and grandchildren.

Get in touch with Elena at mirran.books@gmail.com

NOTES

Chapter 1

1. Haiduc: literally "outlaw". In popular usage, a person who is always busy doing good work.

Chapter 18

1. A notorious miser in a novel by Romanian writer Stefanescu-Delavrancea Barbu (1858-1918)

Milton Keynes UK
Ingram Content Group UK Ltd.
UKHW040628240924
1818UKWH00017B/120